POPULATION GROWTH AND UNEMPLOYMENT IN INDIA BY CASTE: PATH ANALYSIS

UNEMPLOYMENT BY CASTE

N.R. PRABHAKARA

Population Growth and Unemployment in India By Caste: Path Analysis
Copyright © 2024 by N.R. Prabhakara

Library of Congress Control Number: 2024923485

ISBN
979-8-89641-003-4 (Paperback)
979-8-89641-004-1 (eBook)
979-8-89641-002-7 (Hardcover)

Dedicated to My Wife Padma Latha,
My Son Mohan Ram,
My Daughter-in-Law Preeti
and my Grandson Vishva.

TABLE OF CONTENTS

ABSTRACT

In India the caste system has been a large part of society. In addition to secondary evidence based on recent literature analyzing the relevance and impact of the caste system on poverty. The problem of unemployment means the problem of providing work for those who are willing to work. There are many people who are either partly employed or wholly unemployed. It is a well-known fact that India is a thickly populated country. In the mainstream of economic theory, unemployment and under-employment on a vast scale are regarded as a primary cause of poverty.....[1] In economic terminology, waste of labor is commonly discussed as 'unemployment' and 'under-employment'. Together the unemployed and under-employed are assumed to constitute a reservoir of untapped productive potential. This potential can be used to eliminate poverty. The supreme taste of planning is this to channelize the unemployed and under-employed into productive work, which in turn, helps to reduce poverty. The social system in India used to be a cause for increasing unemployment. The joint family system made it impossible for many semi-educated young men to live on the common family income. Finally, the caste system, based on profession, created artificial barriers that prevented the easy transfer of the unemployed from one caste to seek opportunities in another. The caste system seems to have played a large part in creating poverty in India.

---

[1] Myrdal Gunhar, An Approach to Asian Drama, New York, Vintage Books, 1970, p. 962.

CHAPTER 1

INTRODUCTION

The caste system in India has existed for thousands of years and operates by dividing society into hierarchical groups by birth, with the hierarchy being defined on a purity scale. Despite many problems, the caste system has operated successfully for centuries, providing goods and services to India's many millions of citizens. The caste functions as a closed group whose members are restricted in their choice of occupation and degree of social interaction. The growth of urbanization (an estimated 26% of the population now live in cities) is having a far reaching, effects on caste practices, not only in cities but also in villages. In the mainstream of economic theory, unemployment and under-employment on a vast scale are regarded as a primary cause of poverty. In economic terminology, waste of labor is commonly discussed as 'unemployment' and 'under-employment'. Together the unemployed and under-employed are assumed to constitute a reservoir of untapped productive potential. This potential can be used to eliminate poverty. The supreme taste of planning is this to channelize the unemployed and under-employed into productive work, which in turn, helps to reduce poverty.

Poverty in the early years of planning was seen as a product of under development of the economy, a situation arising out of inadequate capital formation. Capital formation depends on the supply of capital and demand for capital. The problem of unemployment is mainly an economic one. In the Indian context five-year plans regularly gave a prominent place to creation of conditions for full employment to make use the potential available. But the commentator of the third plan observed that, though employment targets have even low, performance has failed to live up to expectations. It was further stated that the plan is insufficiently bold in its attack on under- employment.[2] The emphasis in the successive rounds of planning has undergone modification and so also the terminology used.

Chronic poverty describes people (individuals, households, social groups, geographical areas and territories) who are poor for significant periods of their lives, who may pass their poverty on to their children and for whom finding exit routes from poverty is difficult. Large proportions of those who are poor in India are stuck in poverty or are chronically poor. The very size of the problem combined with the fact that many of them will remain poor over time. The concept of unemployment and under-employment have undergone many changes in modern economic theories. The term under-employment and its many synonyms -'hidden', 'concealed', 'invisible', 'disguised', 'potential', and 'latent' unemployment are used by various authors] based on the context in which it is used. In the Indian context, the data is available on under-employment/unemployment through N.S.S data. The present book makes use of the data available in N.S.S. Reports. The study focuses on the data on unemployment and employment.

Unemployment means a state of affair in which, for various reasons, men must remain without jobs over many months or even several years. In this sense, the problem of unemployment in India is essentially the same as in the developed countries of Europe and America. But there are aspects of unemployment in India which are materially different from which we find in the west. Rural poverty has got concentrated in a few inaccessible and less developed areas and those with high incidence of socially disadvantaged population. Urban poverty, however, is high not only in backward areas/ states but many of the developed states. Incidence of urban poverty can thus be attributed to lack of development.

Employment and unemployment scenario is characterized by relative stability in worker population ratio (for working age population) with a slight declining trend over the year. The relative stability and minor changes in unemployment rate despite violent fluctuations in income growth, suggests that employment in organized sector is protected by the system of legislated benefits, those in unorganized sector cannot afford unemployment due to their poor economic conditions. In the industrially advanced countries, the most common type of unemployment to be found can be attributed to a fall in the effective demand for goods and services, or more precisely, to the inability of this demand to keep pace with the increase in working population. In these countries, an increase in population is an addition to the labor force and not to the ranks of unemployed. If it adds to unemployment, it can be corrected by an increase in the demand for goods. Sometimes there is a failure of demand, but there are means by which it can be adjusted upward. There is also another

---

[2]   I.M.D. Little "A Critical Examinations of India's Third Five Year Plan, Oxford Economic Papers, Vol. 14, No. 1, Feb. 1962, p.24.

type of unemployment which results from workers moving from one type of job to another. This is frictional unemployment caused by changes in the industrial structure which are constantly occurring, because of the adoption of new machinery and techniques and as a result of demand shifting from one product to another. But the volume of such unemployment and its duration have been considerably reduced.

In India, the problem is different. Our existing agricultural base and our industrial and commercial super structure are not adequate for offering useful employment opportunities to more people. The new hands that are added as the result of increasing population do not add to our output. Either they are unemployed; or they displace others who are employed; or they share employment with others so that there is more of part time in place of full-time employment or it so happens that work previously done by one person is now done by two or three persons.[3] The special feature of unemployment problem in India is thus the state of chronic involuntary idleness especially among two important section of the population, namely, the agricultural class and the educated middle class. The unbelievable poverty of the Indian people is the consequences of general unemployment and chronic under- employment.

The caste system seems to have played a large part in creating poverty in India. There is a large amount of literature on poverty and the caste system in India. The source often describes the link between the two. There are also many sources solely focused on poverty and solely focused on the caste system in India without linking them. It should be considered to explain why poverty is much more prevalent among the Scheduled Caste and Scheduled Tribes, then among the nonscheduled households, we decompose the difference in the poverty rates between the Scheduled Castes (or Tribes) and non-scheduled households into a part explained by the differences in characteristics (characteristics effect). The Scheduled Caste comprise an important demographic strength in India. The Scheduled Caste population in 2001 was 166.6 million, and in the year 2011 201.4 million. The total Scheduled Caste population constitutes 16.6 percent in 2011. In India, the decadal growth of SC in 2011 was 30.2 per cent, which is more than decadal growth of general population.

About 81 percent of the Scheduled Caste population live in rural areas. About 84 percent of the Scheduled Caste population live in ten states of India. India is the fourth largest economy in terms of GDP valued in PPP (purchasing power parity). India has the largest number of poor people in the world, at an estimated 301.7 million in 2004-05, or 27.5% of the population.

---

[3]   B N Ganguli, Population and Development, S Chand and Co.,(Pvt.) Limited, New Delhi (1973),p.10.

Table 1

Poverty trends, 1973-74 to 2004-05

YEAR	% OF POPULATION BELOW POVERTY	TOTAL POPULATION IN POVERTY (MILLION)
1973-74	54.9	321.3
1977-78	51.3	328.9
1983	44.5	322.9
1987-88	38.9	307.1
1993-94	36.0	320.3
1999-00	26.1	260.2
2004-05	27.5	301.7

• Source: Planning Commission (1997); Press International Bureau (2001, 2007).

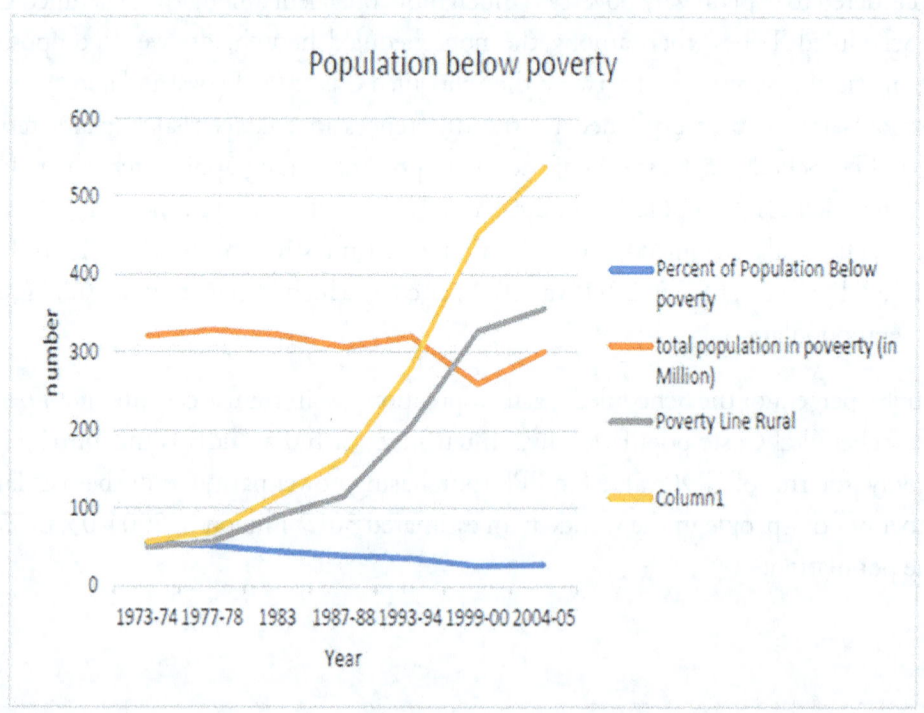

Estimates of poverty are based on a poverty line that is set abysmally low, at Rs 356.30 per capita per month in rural areas and Rs 538.60 per capita per month in urban areas.[4] Meanwhile, poverty declined by 12.4 percentage points over the decade from 1977-78 to 1987-88, but by only 8.5 percentage points between 1993-94 and 2004-05. Overall, the caste system is one of the factors that has contributed to poverty as well as complicated the process of alleviating poverty in India. The sociological factors such as joint family, caste system and Hindu religious values on economic development in India. South Asia is one of the most poverty ridden regions in the world. Although the poverty rate (defined as the percent of people living below $1.25 a day) has decreased from about 60 percent in 1980 to 51.7 percent in 1990 and to 40.3 percent in 2004, there were still about 600 million poor people trying to make a living in South Asia. Specifically, in India, there are still 350 million people who live on less than one dollar a day (Waldman, 2005). As of (2005) the country, who live on less than one dollar a day (Waldman, 2005). As of 2005, the country ranks 127th out of 177 countries on the United Nations Human Development Index (HDI), which measures life span, education and living standard.

Nearly half of India's children are undernourished, a level worse than sub-Saharan Africa. These horrible conditions are magnified by the fact that India has such a large population (over 1.2 billion people), which is growing at 1.4 percent a year. This adds more competition to the workforce as well as putting extra strain on families by forcing them to provide for more people. Although this is a factor in the continuing poverty in India, the caste system that had been present for hundreds of years had a large role in creating these poverty rates.

The **caste system in India** is the paradigmatic ethnographic example of caste. It has origins in ancient India, and was transformed by various ruling elites in medieval, early-modern, and modern India, especially the Mughal Empire and the British Raj. It is today the basis of affirmative action programs in India. The caste system consists of two different concepts, *varna* and *jati*, which may be regarded as different levels of analysis of this system.

The caste system as it exists today is thought to be the result of developments during the collapse of the Mughal era and the rise of the British colonial government in India. The collapse of the Mughal era saw the rise of powerful men who associated themselves with kings, priests and ascetics, affirming the regal and martial form of the caste ideal, and it also reshaped many apparently casteless social groups into differentiated caste communities. The British Raj furthered this development, making

---

[4]   These numbers are based on national official poverty lines specified in respective years.

rigid caste organization a central mechanism of administration. Between 1860 and 1920, the British formulated the caste system into their system of governance, granting administrative jobs and senior appointments only to <u>Christians</u> and people belonging to certain castes. Social unrest during the 1920s led to a change in this policy. From then on, the colonial administration began a policy of <u>positive discrimination</u> by <u>reserving</u> a certain percentage of government jobs for the lower castes. In 1948, negative discrimination on the basis of caste was banned by law and further enshrined in the <u>Indian constitution</u>; however, the system continues to be practiced in parts of India.

The Caste System

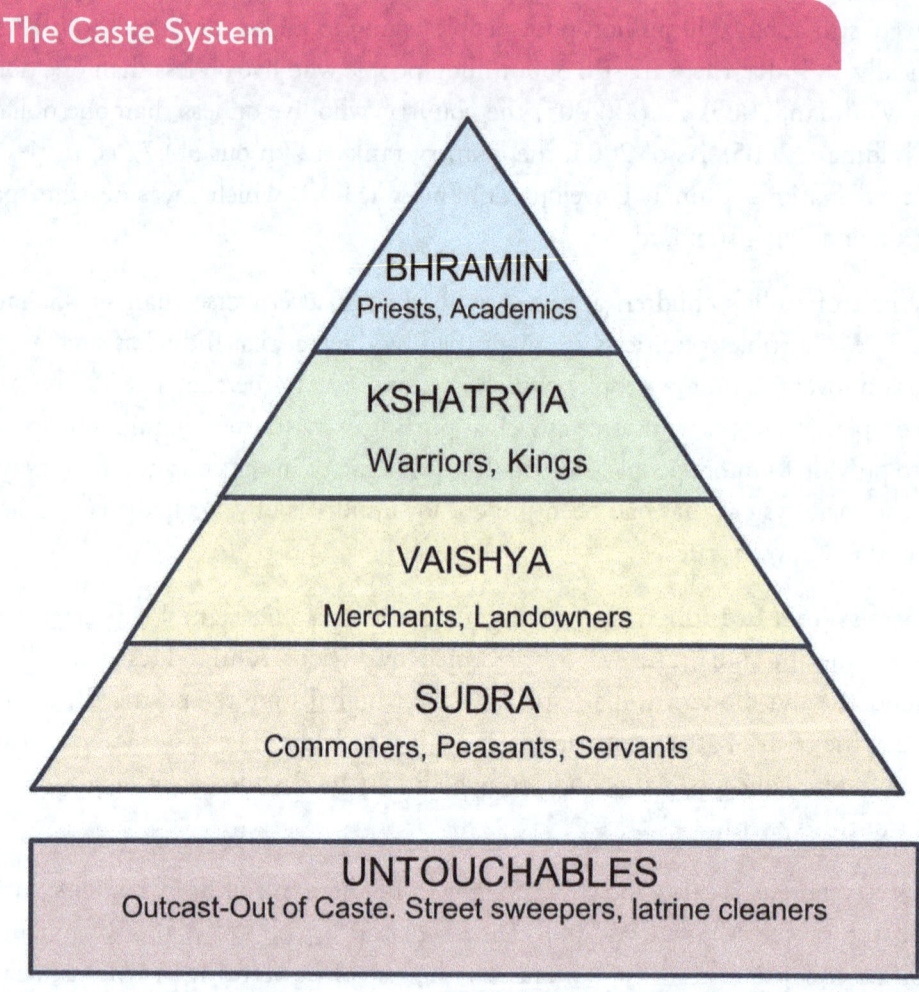

Caste is a form of social stratification characterized by endogamy, hereditary transmission of a style of life which often includes an occupation, ritual status in a hierarchy, and customary social interaction and exclusion based on cultural notions of purity and pollution. Its paradigmatic ethnographic example is the division of India's Hindu society into rigid social groups, with roots in India's ancient history and persisting to the present time. However, the economic significance of the caste system in India has been declining because of urbanization and affirmative action programs. A subject of much scholarship by sociologists and anthropologists, the Hindu caste system is sometimes used as an analogical basis for the study of caste-like social divisions existing outside Hinduism and India.

Although many other nations are characterized by social inequality, perhaps nowhere else in the world has inequality been so elaborately constructed as in the Indian institution of caste. Caste has long existed in India, but in the modern period it has been severely criticized by both Indian and foreign observers. Although some educated Indians tell non-Indians that caste has been abolished or that "no one pays attention to caste anymore," such statements do not reflect reality. [Source: Library of Congress, 1995*].

The caste system is technically illegal but widely practiced (generally more in rural areas). The Hindu social division system comprises four major categories (varnas) that are found India-wide but are often subdivided into hundreds of sub-categories (jatis), many of which are often found only in specific areas. Similar hereditary and occupational social hierarchies exist within Sikh and Muslim communities but are generally far less pervasive and institutionalized. About 16 percent of the total population is "untouchable" (Scheduled Castes is the more formal, legal term; Dalit is the term preferred by "untouchables" and roughly translates to downtrodden); around 8 percent of the population belongs to one of 461 indigenous groups (often called Scheduled Tribes for legal purposes, although the term Adivasi is commonly used). [Source: Library of Congress, 2005] Five major principals define the caste system: 1) marriage within one's caste; 2) restrictions on eating and drinking within caste; 3) hereditary membership to a caste; 4) the association of specific castes with specific occupations; and 5) the ranking of castes into a hierarchy. The caste system seems to contradict the idea that all men are created equal—an important concept in Buddhism, Islam and Christianity

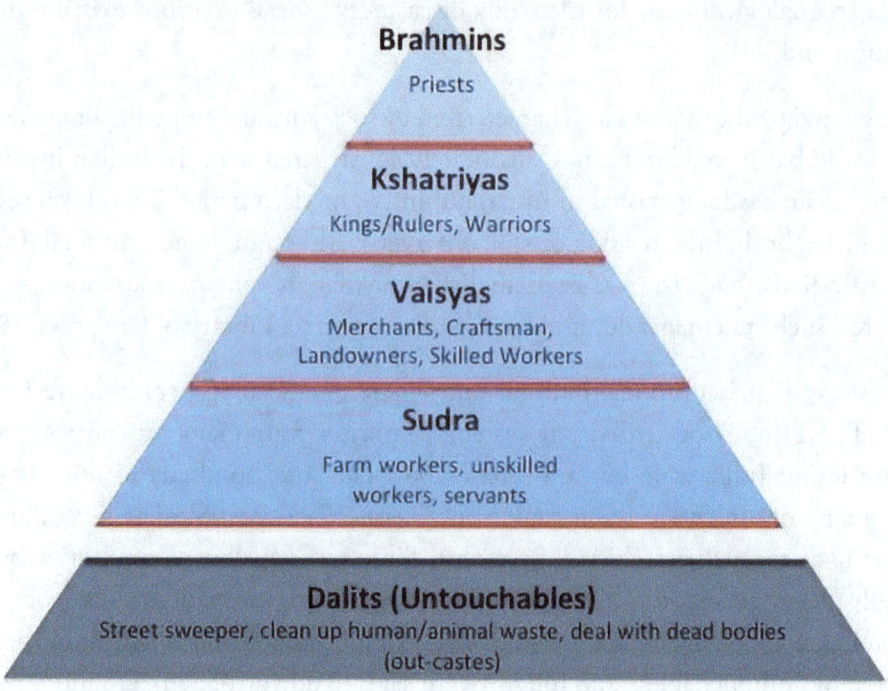

In <u>South Asia</u> the <u>caste</u> system has been a dominating aspect of social organization for thousands of years. A caste, generally designated by the term *jati* ("birth"), refers to a strictly regulated social <u>community</u> into which one is born. Some *jati*s have occupational names, but the connection between caste and occupational specialization is limited. In general, a person is expected to <u>marry</u> someone within the same *jati*, follow a particular set of rules for proper behavior (in such matters as kinship, occupation, and diet), and interact with other *jati*s according to the group's position in the social <u>hierarchy</u>. Based on names alone, it is possible to identify more than 2,000 *ja- ti*s. However, it is common for there to be several distinct groups bearing the same name that are not part of the same marriage network or local caste system.

In India virtually all nontribal Hindus and many adherents of other faiths (even Muslims, for whom caste is theoretically anathema) recognize their membership in one of those hereditary social <u>communities</u>. Among Hindus, *jati*s are usually assigned to one of four large caste clusters, called *varna*s, each of which has a traditional social function: <u>Brahmans</u> (priests), at the top of the social hierarchy, and, in descending <u>prestige</u>, <u>Kshatriyas</u> (warriors), <u>Vaishyas</u> (originally peasants but later merchants), and <u>Shudras</u> (artisans and laborers). The particular *varna* in which a *jati* is ranked depends in part on its relative level of "impurity," determined by the group's traditional contact with any of a number of "pollutants," including blood, menstrual flow, saliva, dung, leather, dirt, and hair. Inter caste restrictions were established to prevent the relative purity of a particular *jati* from being corrupted by the pollution of a lower caste. A fifth group, the Panchama's (from Sanskrit *panch*, "five"), theoretically were excluded from the system because their occupations and ways of life typically brought them in contact with such impurities. They were formerly called the untouchables (because their touch, believed by the upper castes to transmit pollution, was avoided), but the nationalist leader Mohandas (Mahatma) Gandhi referred to them as Harijan ("Children of God"), a name that for a time gained popular usage. More recently, members of that class have adopted the term Dalit ("Oppressed") to describe themselves. Officially, such groups are referred to as Scheduled Castes. Those in Scheduled Castes, collectively accounting for roughly one-sixth of India's total population, are generally landless and perform most of the agricultural labor, as well as a number of ritually polluting caste occupations (e.g., leatherwork, among the Chamars, the largest Scheduled Caste).

India's many tribal peoples—officially designated as Scheduled Tribes—have also been given status similar to that of the Scheduled Castes. Tribal peoples are concentrated mainly in the northeast (notably Meghalaya, Mizoram, and Nagaland) and, to a lesser extent, in the northeastcentral (Chhattisgarh, Jharkhand, and Odisha) regions of the country, as well as in the Lakshadweep and Dadra and Nagar Haveli union territories.

While inherently nonegalitarian, *jatis* provide Indians with social support and, at least in theory, a sense of having a secure and well-defined social and economic role. In most parts of India, there is one or perhaps there are several dominant castes that own the majority of land, are politically most powerful, and set a cultural tone for a particular region. A dominant *jati* typically forms anywhere from one-eighth to one-third of the total rural population but may in some areas account for a clear majority (e.g., Sikh Jats in central Punjab, Marathas in parts of Maharashtra, or Rajput's in northwestern Uttar Pradesh). The second most numerous *jati* is usually from one of the Scheduled Castes. Depending on its size, a village typically will have between 5 and 25 *jatis*, each of which might be represented by anywhere from 1 to more than 100 households.

CHAPTER 2

EMPLOYMENT SITUATIONS IN THE COUNTRY

Unemployment and under-employment constitute the greatest social problems in India today. On account, of the rapid growth of population, there is a large and growing labor force to be absorbed into gainful economic activity and poverty is the inevitable consequences of large-scale unemployment and under-employment. But in the context of the socio-economic conditions prevailing in our country, the problem of defining and measuring employment, and unemployment or under-employment becomes difficult and, therefore, reliable estimates of unemployment have not been hitherto available.

The authentic data source of employment/unemployment indicators in India at present is the Periodic Labor Fource Survey (PLFS) conducted by the Ministry of Statistics and Pregame Implementation since 2017-18. The annual PLFS reports for the years 2017-18, 2018-19,2019-20, 2020-21 and 2021-22 are available in the pubic domine. Prior to PLF's i.e., before 2017-18, National Statistical Office (NSO), Ministry of Statistics and Program Implementation, used to conduct quinquennial Employment and Unemployment surveys. The last such survey was done in the year 2011-12.

· Employment data based on PLFS Report:

The PLFS (Periodic Labor Force Survey) aims to provide *quarterly changes* of various indicators of Labor Market for urban areas and its annual estimates of different labor force indicators for both rural as well as urban areas at State/UT and all India level. The survey period of PFS survey is 1st July to 30th June of next year.

As per annual PLFS report, the Labor Force participation Rate (LFPR), Worker Population Ratio (WPR) and Unemployment Rate (UR) in usual status for person of age 15 years and above were as follows.

Table 2

Unemployment rate 2017-22 (in percentage)

YEAR	WPR	LFPR	UR
2017-18	46.8	49.8	6.0
2018-19	47.3	50.2	5.8
2019-20	50.9	53.5	4.8
2020-21	52.6	54.9	4.2
2021-22	52.9	55.2	4.1

- **Source: Periodic Labor Force Survey; 2022-23, New Delhi, India.**

The above table indicates that the Labor Force and work Force in the country increased steadily and on the other hand Unemployment Rate has declined.

The comparison of 27th round and 32nd round of the National Sample Survey with 61st round with 64th round of National Sample Survey was largely devoted to a survey of employment- unemployment situation in the country. The number of sample households for the social groups Scheduled caste (SC), Scheduled tribes (ST), other backward class (OBC) and others, at all India was 16203, 20284, 46348 and 41759 respectively. In this work, estimates of the employment– unemployment indicators for various social groups have been presented with respect to the usual status. Unemployment is one field where the need for more accurate and reliable information has long been most keenly felt. As it is stated "The best route to poverty in all aviation is to increase the productivity of the poor- that is, to reduce their unemployment and under-employment and increase their efficiency. Poverty conceived development is essentially a "plus-sum" process in which most participants benefit not a "zero-sum" process in which one participant gain in another loss.....[5] In this scene, the problem of unemployment in our country is essentially the same as in the developed countries of Europe and America, "Statistics of unemployment are not just statistics..... Statistics of unemployment mean rows of men and women, not of figures only."

Table 3

• **Unemployment Rate in India: Historical Data**

YEAR	UNEMPLOYMENT RATE (PERCENT)
2024	9.2
2023	8.003
2022	7.33
2021	5.98
2020	8.0
2019	5.27
2018	5.33
2017	5.36
2016	5.42
2015	5.44
2014	5.44
2013	5.42
2012	5.41

---

[5]   Barend A de Varies, (1981), Public Policy and the Private Sector,Economic Development and the Private Sector, IMF and World Bank, Washington.

2011	5.43
2010	5.55
2009	5.44
2008	5.41

- **Source: Periodic Labor Force Survey Report.**

The number of unemployment as measured in 1961 census was 45,068 as against 81,400 in 1971 census. In both the years the proportion of unemployment to total population was higher in urban areas as compared to rural areas and higher among males in both the urban and rural areas. Based on the 64th round survey on employment and unemployment and migration particulars conducted during July 2007 to June 2008. The survey covered a sample of 1,25,578 households (79,091 in rural areas and 46,487 in urban areas) and a sample of 5,72,254 persons (3,74,294 in rural areas and 1,97,960 in urban areas). Employment and unemployment rates were measured in three different approach, viz. Usual status (us) with a reference period of one-year, current weekly status (cws) with a one-week reference period and current daily status (cds) based on the daily activity pursued during each day of the reference week.

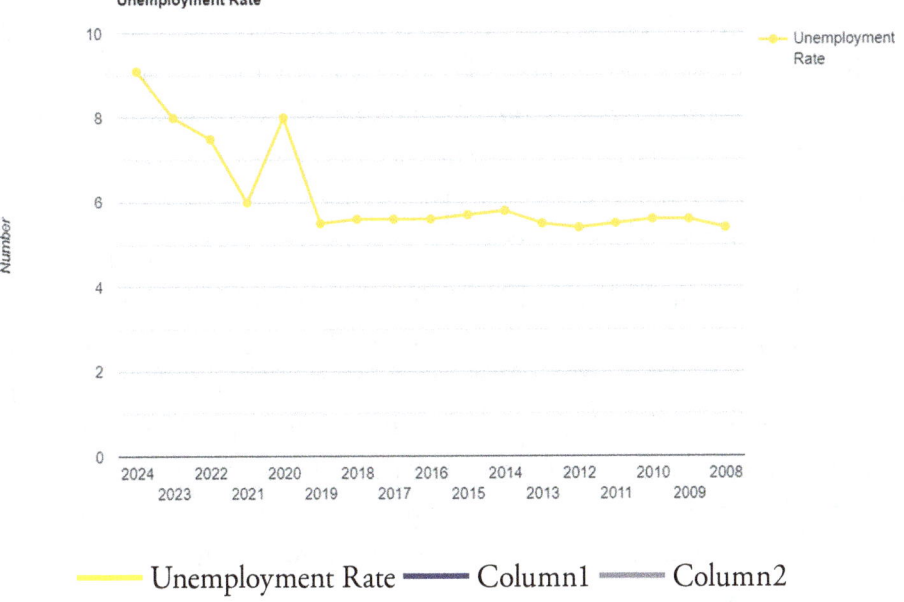

- Fig: Unemployment rate 2024-2008.

Unlike in earlier plans, in the fourth five-year plan there was no specific mention of the target for creation of employment opportunities. Thus, there was no estimates of the backlog of unemployment at the beginning of the fourth plan, no estimates of the increase in the labor force during the plan period and no estimates of additional employment likely to be created through the implementation of the fourth plan as formulated. The expert Committee observed that the data available for estimating unemployment and under-employment in the past have not been adequate and that the conclusions based on them were, therefore, unavoidably subject to an unknown margin of error.

It is important to recognize in this context that many of the limitations of the estimates of labor force, employment and unemployment are inherent in the socio-economic conditions in our country and cannot overcome by conceptual refinements of techniques of estimations. The socioeconomic situation in India, it is not possible to have precise estimates of employment and unemployment. In this context we examine the nature of the empirical data being made available during the last five decades through continuous large-scale sample surveys into the employment and level of living of people in rural and urban areas. Attention will be confined to only two problems: namely the extent of change in employment and the level of living of the population.

Segregation can become quite intense when the whole society puts its mind to it. The struggle with huge poverty, social classes vie for resources. And the existence of very specific classes in India helps this process. In a way the causes of poverty. Urbanization in India partly rely on social structure and relations. This creates discrimination that generates an "artificial" poverty between castes and genders, between religion and tribes. Likewise, in many case the situation of women and their bottom-low in India partly rely on social structure and relations. This creates discrimination that generates an "artificial" poverty between castes and genders, between religion and tribes. Likewise, in many cases the situation of women and their bottom-low participation in the economy among Asian countries counts as one more issue among the cause of poverty in India.

Based on classification of individual member of households by usual activity status percentage estimates of the number of persons chronically unemployed have been obtained separately for rural and urban areas, taking the total rural and urban population as base. In the rural areas, normally very few people report as usually not having any gainful work and openly seeking or available for employment. Nevertheless, the figures of unemployed persons thrown up by the survey data are not so small as can be dismissed as insignificant as can be seen from the following Table 4.

Table 4

Percentage of Population Chronically Unemployed in India 2011-12

RURAL	Male	0.59
	Female	0.16
	Total	0.38
URBAN	Male	2.93
	Female	0.86
	Total	1.93

- **Source: NSS Report on Employment & Unemployment Situation in India 2011-12 (68th Round)**

The picture of unemployment in different States is shown in Table 3. The sex ratio of population may be expressed as the number of females per thousand males. It is a basic demographic determinant of population change. Sex composition of population directly influences proportion of married persons in a population and birth rate, and it indirectly influences supply of labor. Among various elements of population composition, sex ratio holds a prime place for population geographers. The sex ratio was an index of economy prevailing in an area and was useful tool for regional analysis. Sex composition is an index of the socio-economic conditions of an area. It is an important tool for regional analysis, and it is a subject of great interest. Thus, the study of sex ratio is essential for understanding the employment and consumption patterns, and social need of a community.

The scheduled castes constituting about 16.2 percent of the country's population represent historically disadvantaged sections of society. To begin with however, we look at the f/m (0-4) and f/m (5-9) figures at the state level for the urban as well as the rural population. The f/m values in the 0-4 age group are an outcome of a mixed pattern of excess male mortality during infancy and the excess female child mortality during the next four years of life. The stronger the inequality, the larger is the excess female child mortality. When examining the caste system effect in India, the pattern that exist can be linked to poverty. The people in lower castes are assigned menial jobs. This helps to explain why there is so much poverty. These lower caste members are not allowed to move up the career ladder and instead remain poor. There also are additional country-specific restrictions with various degrees that further the exclusion-poverty cycle. By bringing the socially excluded into mainstream society, and ensuring their fundamental human rights in the process, they are likely to help overcome poverty and deprivation among the disadvantaged in society.

The caste system in India has existed for thousands of years and operates by dividing society into hierarchical groups by birth, with the hierarchy being defined on a purity scale. The percentage of rural population working and available for work to total population in India is 0.28 which amounts to 0.75 million in actual numbers. It is 2.43 for Kerala and 0.52 for All India. The situation in urban areas is worse. The percentage of total urban population classified as unemployed (persons seeking and available) is 1.93 in Karnataka (1.23 lakhs). It is 2.05 for all India, 4.92 for Kerala, 3.53 for West Bengal, 2.83 for Andhra Pradesh, 2.50 for Tamil Nadu, 2.18 for Orissa and 2.01 for Maharashtra. The percentage of such people in Karnataka can be termed as moderately high. However, for obvious reasons, the real impact of unemployment is felt more by the male population.

Table 5

· **Unemployment Rates by States 2011-12.**

SL. NO.	STATES	UNEMPLOYMENT RATES (PERCENT)
1	Kerala	26.02
2	Tamil Nadu	16.06
3	Andhra Pradesh	10.78
4	West Bengal	10.44
5	Karnataka	9.58
6	Orissa	8.16
7	Maharashtra	8.15
8	Bihar	8.13

9	Haryana	6.87
10	Gujarat	6.38
11	Chandigarh	5.55
12	Punjab	5.03
13	Uttara Pradesh	4.29
14	Rajasthan	3.55
15	Madhya Pradesh	3.13
16	Himachal Pradesh	2.19
17	Meghalaya	2.50
18	Assam	1.82
19	Nagaland	0.52
20	Manipur	N.A.
21	Tripura	N.A.
22	Arunachal Pradesh	N.A.
23	Mizoram	N.A.

- **Source: NSS Report 2011-12 (68ᵗh Round).**

The Scheduled Caste population in India, according to the 2001 Census was 166,635,700 persons, constitute 16.2 per cent of the India's total population. About 79.8 per cent (four fifth) and 20.2 per cent (one fifth) of the population live in rural and urban areas respectively. In India more than 57 percent of total Scheduled Castes population live in these five States. The highest percentage (21.1 percent) of Scheduled Caste population to the total Scheduled Caste population of the country live in Uttar Pradesh, in West Bengal 11.1 per cent and in Bihar 7.8 per cent, in Andhra Pradesh 7.4 percent and in Tamil Nadu 7.1 percent. The largest proportion of population of the Scheduled Castes to total population of the State is in Punjab i.e., 28.9 percent, followed by Himachal Pradesh, 24.7 percent and in West Bengal 23 percent. In Andhra Pradesh, Karnataka and Pondicherry population of Scheduled Caste population is equal to the National

Average of 16.2 percent. In the North-Eastern tribal States such as Mizoram only 272 persons, followed by Meghalaya 0.5 percent and in Arunachal Pradesh 0.6 percent is the smallest concentration of the Scheduled Caste population.

Applying the rate of unemployment (percentage of the total population) to projected population for 1973.[6] An estimate of the total number of usually or chronically unemployed persons has been built-up. The estimated total number of unemployed persons has reached the level of 1.98 lakhs (0.75 lakhs in rural areas and 1.23 lakhs in urban areas) in 1972-73 in Karnataka. For the whole of India, the number is 40.72 lakhs (19.91 lakhs in rural areas and 20.81 lakhs in urban areas). Karnataka thus accounts for about one-twenty of the total number of unemployed persons in the country. Because there is a vast army of under-employed persons in villages and towns. Thus, the problem is more- huge. Some more aspects of the nature and extent of under-employment has been made in the following paragraphs.

Table 6

· **Percentage of Labor Force Chronically Unemployed 2011-12.**

RURAL	Male	0.83
	Female	0.32
	Total	0.65
URBAN	Male	5.04
	Female	4.45
	Total	4.01

• **Source: Statistical Abstract, Karnataka 2011-12.**

Another interesting side light regarding the acuteness of the problem has come to the force from the answers recorded in the survey schedule of the persons usually seeking or available for employment and this is presented below. It is obvious that in rural areas, the percentage of persons making some tangible effort to get employment for about one

---

[6]   Government of Karnataka,Buearo of Economics and Statistics, Population Projections for Mysore, 1972-88, (1973).

year or less is 48.65 of the unemployed persons. Whereas the number of persons seeking for more than one year constitutes 51.35 percent. In the urban areas of the State 56.32 per cent of the total unemployed persons were found to be seeking or available for work for more than one year, as compared to 45.53 per cent for all India. This proportion was 58.86 per cent in Kerala, 56.91 per cent in Tamil Nadu, 53.15 percent in Andhra Pradesh and 43.51 per cent in Maharashtra. A more precise and meaningful indicators (from the point of view of policy pressures) of the measure of chronic unemployment can be obtained by expressing the number of usually unemployed persons as percentages of persons in labor force (which largely excludes children's and old). The immensity of the problem can be properly realized if the rates for both male and female population in the labor force in rural and urban areas are examined as shown below. A comparative picture of the percentage of people seeking and available work to total labor force in different States is given in Table 7.

Unemployment is one of the major problems of India. According to 2011 census 788 million (15-60 Years) is the work force and unemployed force of India constitutes 113 million persons from 70 million families (28 percent families of the nation) whereas about 23 percent according to 2001 Census. This shows an increase of 28 percent within 10 years. The magnitude of unemployment in India differs from religion to religion. In India according to 2011, 47 million (20 percent) of youth between age group 15-24 years were unemployed and seeking employment.

Table 7

- ### Percentage of People Seeking and Available for work to total Labor Force

		SEEKING EMPLOYMENT			AVAILABLE FOR EMPLOYMENT		
		Male	Female	Total	Male	Female	Total
1	Andhra Pradesh	0.63	0.20	0.45	6.45	7.51	6.75
2	Assam	1.12	2.31	1.30	3.84	7.32	4.09
3	Bihar	2.19	1.19	1.91	5.11	3.96	4.99
4	Gujarat	0.97	0.23	0.68	2.89	2.77	2.87

5	Haryana	1.59	0.19	1.09	4.16	8.44	5.39
6	Jammu & Kashmir	0.37	0.34	0.36	2.43	4.65	2.67
7	Karnataka	0.88	0.32	0.65	5.04	4.45	4.91
8	Kerala	5.79	5.31	5.62	11.21	13.58	12.02
9	Madhya Pradesh	0.13	-	0.08	3.97	3.09	3.91
10	Maharashtra	0.79	0.15	0.51	4.43	6.33	4.80
11	Orissa	1.35	0.58	1.10	5.21	4.98	5.18
12	Punjab	0.89	0.17	0.68	3.20	7.32	3.93
13	Rajasthan	0.76	0.44	0.62	2.19	1.78	2.03
14	Tamil Nadu	1.41	0.43	0.99	6.28	5.46	6.08
15	Utara Pradesh	0.65	0.28	0.54	2.03	2.19	2.41
16	West Bengal	1.99	3.49	2.27	7.51	15.33	8.45
	All India	1.22	0.63	1.01	4.86	6.47	5.18

- **Source: N.S.S., op. Cit., p.,18.**

The following table gives details about the magnitude of unemployment in India among youths between age groups 20-29 years from different religions.

Table 8

- **Unemployment Percentage of Youth by Religion 20-29 age group.**

India	20
Hindus	20
Muslims	20
Christian	26

Sikh	17
Buddhist	18
Jain	12
Others	35

Even after its impressive performance in the field of science and technology and agriculture during last three four decades a vast majority of Indian people is struggling with problems of poverty and maul nutrition. The economic reforms of 1991, despite spurring a huge growth of the economy, have left the country with terrible inequalities, within cities as well as between rural and urban areas. They were the best opportunities to seriously tackle the cause of poverty in India and more especially rural poverty. With two thirds of the population living in rural areas and some 500 million poor (or more), even urban poverty stems from the rural migration to the city.

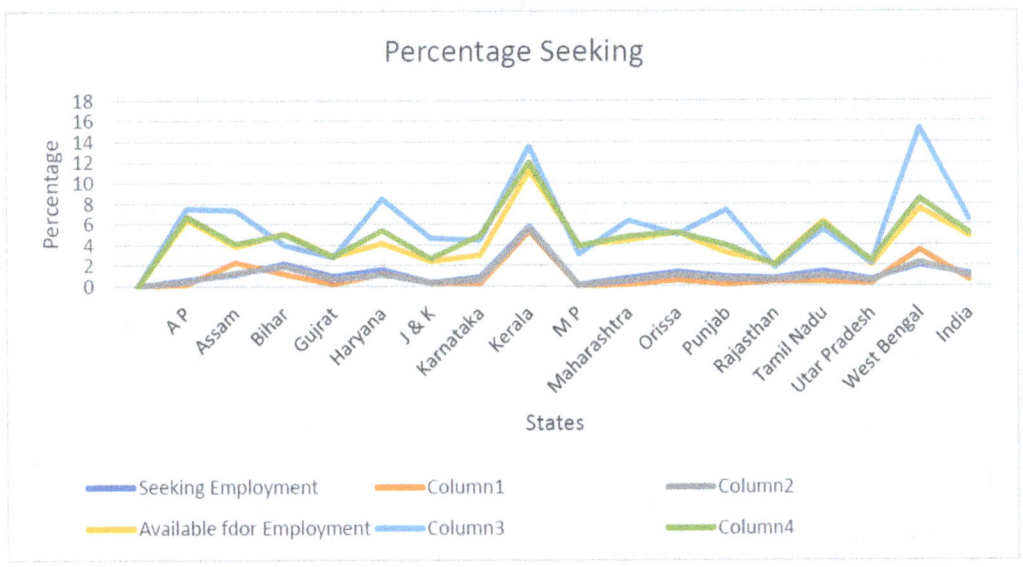

During the period 2004-05, 2009-10, and 2011-12 the percentage of unemployment rate in rural males varied between 1.6 percent and 1.7 percent. This variation was 1.1 percent and 1.3 percent among ST's and 1.7 percent between 1.6 percent and 1.7 percent. This variation was 1.1 percent and 1.3 percent among ST's and 1.7 percent and 2.0 percent among SC's the percentage rate is high among SC's than ST's. The unemployment rate among rural females varied between 1.6 percent and 1.8 percent. Among ST's this was 0.4 percent and 1.1 percent whereas among SC's it was 1.4 percent and 1.5 percent during the period. The rate among SC's is more than ST's. The unemployment rate among urban males varied between 2.8 percent and 3.8 percent which was 2.9 percent and 4.4 percent among male ST's and 3.1 and 5.5 percent among male SC's and the rate is higher in SC's than ST's. The unemployment rate among urban females varied between 5.2 percent and 6.9 percent which was 3.4 percent and 4.8 percent among males ST's and 4.2 percent and 4.6 percent among male SC's and the rate is higher in ST's than SC's. The following table gives details.

Table 9

· Unemployment rate by Sex, Rural/Urban 2004-2012. (in percent)

YEAR	ST	SC	OBC	OTHERS	TOTAL
RURAL MALE					
2011-12	1.3	2.0	1.7	1.8	1.7
2009-10	1.7	1.7	1.4	2.0	1.6
2004-05	1.1	1.7	1.5	2.0	1.6
RURAL FEMALE					
2011-12	1.1	1.4	1.7	2.4	1.7
2009-10	0.9	1.5	1.4	2.5	1.6
2004-05	0.4	1.4	1.9	2.9	1.8
URBAN MALES					
2011-12	3.4	3.2	2.5	3.4	3.0
2009-10	4.4	3.1	2.8	2.7	2.8
2004-05	2.9	5.5	3.3	3.7	3.8
URBAN FEMALES					
2011-12	4.8	4.5	4.7	6.3	5.2

2009-10	4.3	4.2	6.2	6.2	5.7
2004-05	3.4	4.6	6.7	8.5	6.9

- **Source: NSSO Survey 68ᵗʰ Round, 20/01/2018 Employment: India– Indpaedia.**

It is particularly for the Dalits (150 million people)– ask the Untouchables or Harridans- that things prove difficult. Being the out-caste "caste" (i.e., so low in the social hierarchy that technically they don't belong to any caste), they have never got a chance to work in agriculture. Segregation can become quite intense when the whole society puts its mind to it. In a way, the cause of poverty in India partly relays on social structures and relations. The economic impact of caste has been studied extensively. A study of factoryworkers in Poona (Lambert, 1963) finds evidence of substantial wage discrimination against workers belonging to backward caste groups. Others use data from cotton mills in Bombay (Morris, 1965) and for shoemakers in Agra (Lynch,1965) to find evidence of discrimination. The wage discrimination to be higher than occupation discrimination. All of these studies collect data in non-experimental settings. Hence the disparities they report in wages and occupation choice fail to control fully for differences in productivity and differences in preferences between high and low-caste workers. As a result, they do not provide a direct test of the hypothesis that discrimination is present.:

The planning commission of India say, the poverty among SC, ST, and OBC is declining due to five-year plan's.

Table 10

- **Poverty among SC's and ST's Rural and Urban (in Percentage)**

YEAR	SC		ST		OTHERS		TOTAL	
	Rural	Urban	Rural	Urban	Rural	Urban	Rural	Urban
1983-84	58.1	56.5	63.8	54.2	37.0	39.1	45.6	42.2
1993-94	48.1	49.9	52.2	42.4	31.3	30.6	37.1	33.7

1999-00	36.2	38.6	45.0	34.8	21.6	20.6	27.1	23.7
2004-05	52.7	40.0	61.9	35.0	26.2	15.8	41.8	25.7
2009-10	43.5	33.0	47.1	28.8	21.1	11.9	33.8	20.9

• **Source: GOI,** *Planning Commission. Eleventh Five Year Plan,2007-20012. Volume I, Inclusive Growth and NSSO Primary Data, 2000-10.*

The reason-based study has focused on methods of control that provide an interpretation of the relation between unemployment and poverty. Hypothetically, there could be six causal connections between three variables X1 (Population Growth), X2 (Un employment), and X3 (Poverty), as follows:

Table 11

• Poverty line, 1973-74 to 2004-05

YEAR	RS PER CAPITA PER MONTH CURRENT PRICE	
	RURAL	URBAN
1973-74	49.63	56.76
1977-78	56.84	70.33
1983	89.5	1`15.65
1987-88	115.2	162.16
1993-94	205.84	281.35
1999-00	327.56	454.11
2004-05	356.30	538.60

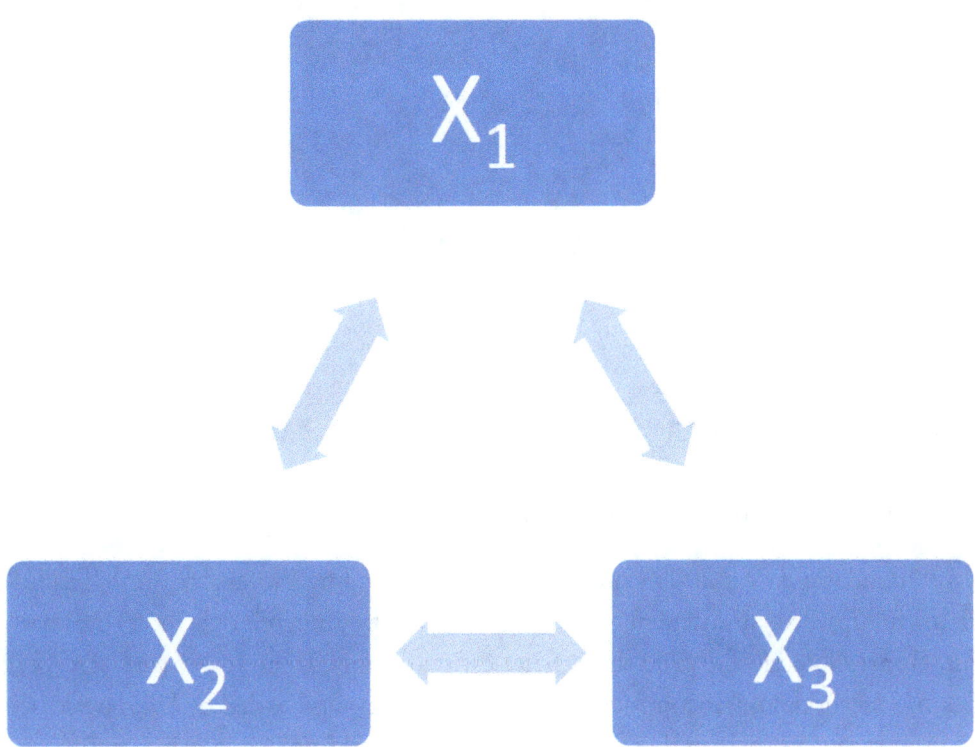

Official poverty estimates are available at the national and state levels for the entire population, but not by social or religious groups, for all years during which the NSSO conducted quinquennial surveys. The Planning Commission has published poverty ratios for the first six of these surveys based on the Lakdawala lines and for the last three based on the Tendulkar lines. These ratios were estimated for rural and urban areas at the national and state level.

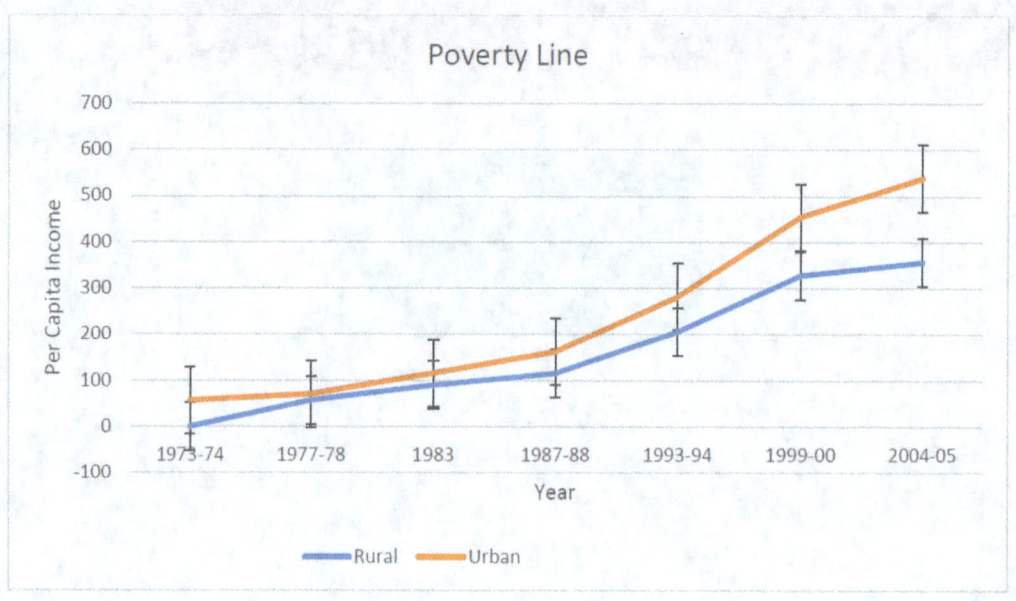

• Source: Economic Survey 2005-2006, Government of India.

Recommendations of a 2009 expert committee headed by Professor Suresh Tendulkar led to an upward adjustment in the rural poverty line relative to its Lakdawala counterpart. Therefore, while the official estimates for earlier year were based on the lines and methodology recommended by the expert group headed by Lakdawala, those for more recent years were based on the line and methodology recommended by the Tendulkar Committee.

Are the issues of socioeconomic inequalities related to specific caste biases in Contemporary India? Why are some social groups in the socioeconomic ladder lagging compared to others? How much have the poor people living in rural areas in India achieved their esteemed goals in the present economic arena of development? Is it the limited educational attainment or lack of physical and social capital of the poor households that begets inter-group economic inequality? Or is it a social identity that impedes the well-being of a certain social group? In search of answering these questions, this article explores the role of castes in explaining socioeconomic inequalities in the rural settings of contemporary India. The limited access to basic amenities and the poor educational attainment of the lower castes and the dominance of the upper castes in these regards show the persistence of social group inequalities. Four remote villages of Purulia district, one of the most backward tribal districts of West Bengal were systematically selected for scrutiny to explore socioeconomic inequality within the caste structure. Two are tribal villages with low inequality and the other two are multi-caste-oriented villages with high inequality.

CHAPTER 3

METHODOLOGY

With two thirds of the population living in rural areas and some 500 million poor (or more), even urban poverty stems from the rural migration to the cities. Here the attempt has been made to study direct and indirect. It can be hypothesized that Ex1 has only an indirect effect on En2. The causes of poverty in India are nothing sort of complex problem. The economic reforms of 1991, despite spurring a huge growth of the economy, have left the country with terrible inequalities, within cities as well as rural and urban areas. They were the best opportunity to seriously tackle the causes of poverty in India and more specifically effects of caste system on poverty and unemployment in India by using Path Analysis. It can be hypothesized that Ex1 has only an indirect effect on En2. The causes of poverty in India are nothing sort of complex problem. The economic reforms of 1991, despite spurring a huge growth of the economy, have left the country with terrible inequalities, within cities as well as rural and urban areas. They were the best opportunity to seriously tackle the causes of poverty in India.

Segregation can become quite intense when the whole society puts its mind to it. The struggle with huge poverty, social classes vie for resources. In causal modeling, the causal interrelationships are examined among a set of variables that have been logically ordered based on time. Thus, in a causal system where X1 (Population Growth) is the independent variable, X2 (Unemployment) the intervening variable, and X3 (Poverty) the dependent variable., X2 cannot cause X1 and X3 cannot cause X2 or X1. With the assumptions, some possible models explicating relations between X1, X2, and X3 are presented here. The first step of path analysis was exemplified in our discussion of patterns of unemployment due to the caste system. A set of coefficients identified as Pig with i being the dependent variable and j the independent variable. These values are *path coefficient.* Thus, P31 is the path coefficient connecting X1 with X3, being determined by X1. Similarly, P4w is the path coefficient linking X4 with residual variable W.

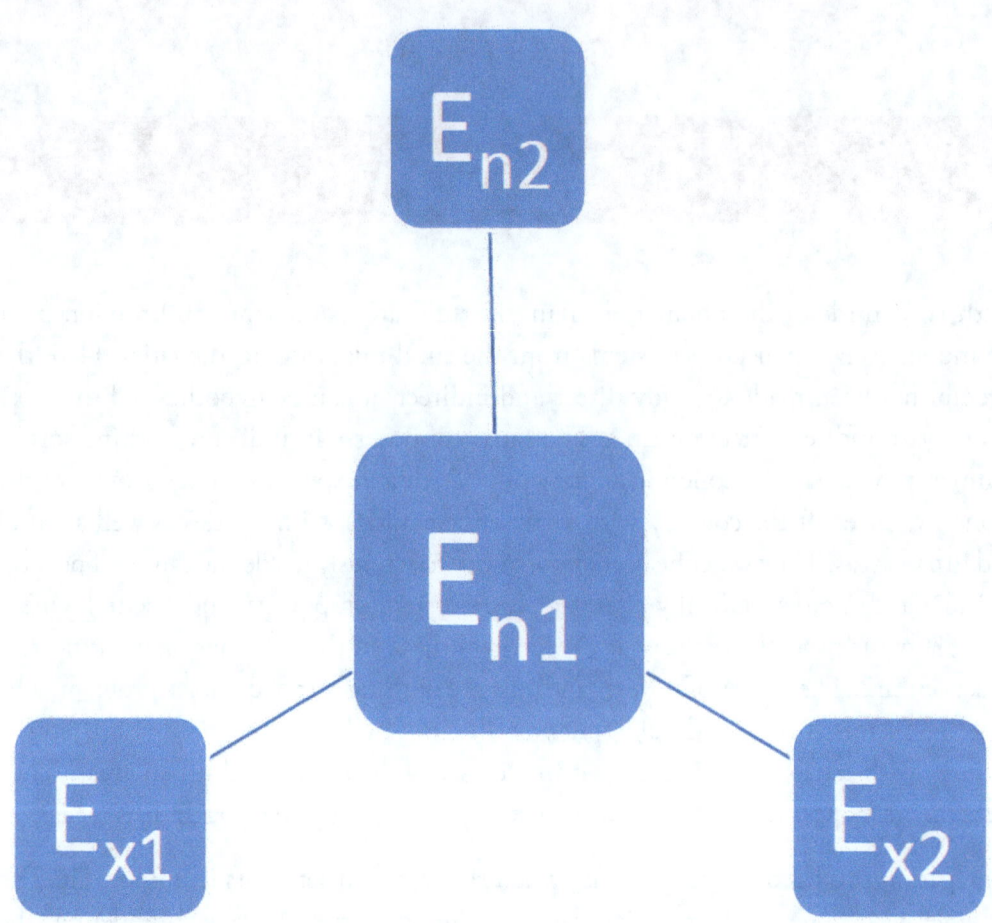

Thus, we test the hypothesis:

1. Poverty and Unemployment has direct effect on population Growth.

2. Caste system creates more Unemployment.

Thus, to represent the structure of the model we have:

*   X2 = P21X1 + P2uU

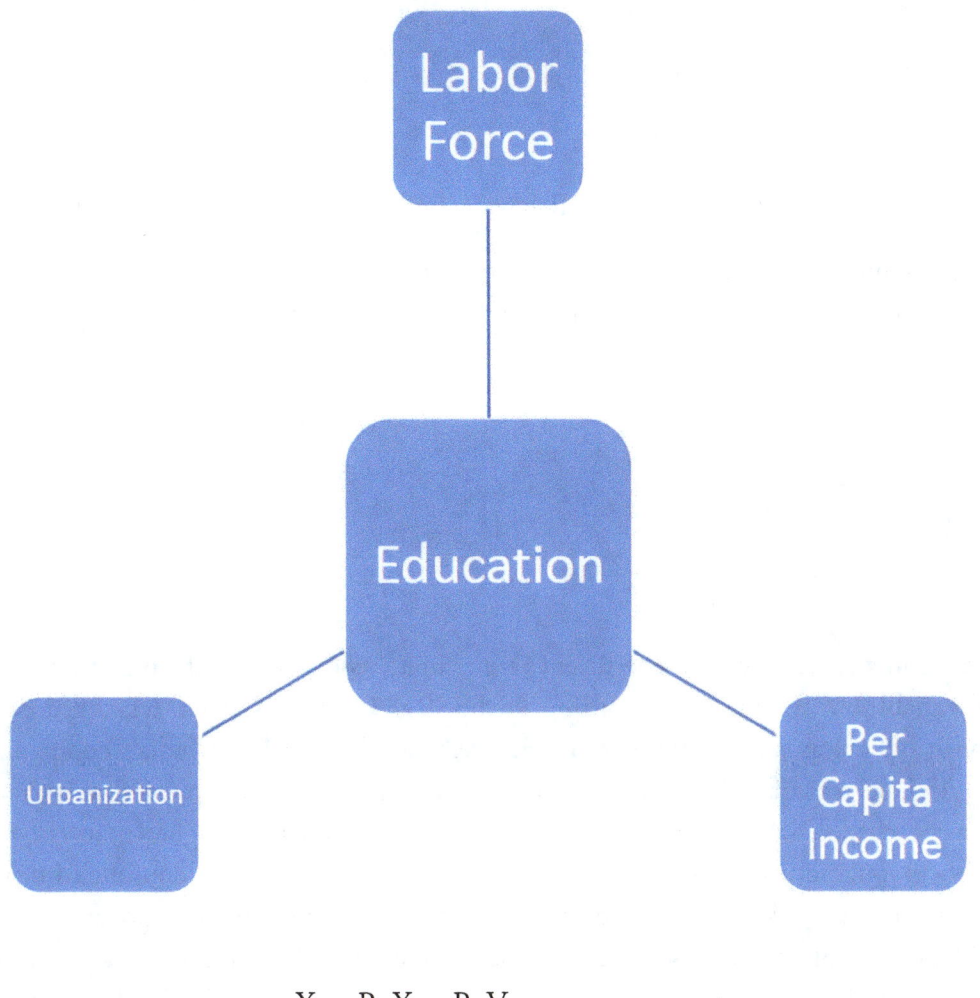

$$X_3 = P_{31}X_1 + P_{3v}V$$

$$X_4 = P_{41}X_1 + P_{42}X_2 + P_{43}X_3 + P_{4w}W$$

Here each equation includes as many terms as there are arrows leading to the dependent variable. Thus, X_4 has four arrows, each representing a determining factor, they are X_1, X_2, X_3, and W.

To obtain estimates of the path coefficient we simply regress each dependent variable on the independent variables in the equation. To estimate P_{21} we regress X_2 to X_1. For P_{31} we regress X_3 on X_1, and for P_{41}, P_{42}, and P_{43} we simply regress X_4 on X_1, X_2, and X_3. Since the variables are standardized the path coefficients are simply the beta weights for each equation. That is:

- $P_{21} = \beta_{21}$ $\qquad$ $P_{42} = \beta_{42}$

- $P_{31} = \beta_{31}$ $\qquad$ $P_{43} = \beta_{43}$

- $P_{41} = \beta_{41}$ $\qquad$ P_{21}

A Path Diagram of Unemployment Behavior

The residual path coefficients (P_{2v}, P_{3v}, P_{4v}) is the square root of the unexplained variations in the dependent variable under analysis. In the case of model presented here are:

- $P_{2v} = \sqrt{(1 - R^2_{2.1})}$

- $P_{3v} = \sqrt{(1 - R^2_{3.1})}$

- $P_{4v} = \sqrt{(1 - R^2_{4.123})}$

The estimation of the path coefficient results in an assessment of the direct effect on all variables in the model. According to the 1991 Census of India, scheduled caste and tribes comprise 16.5 percent and 8.1 percent respectively, of India's population, yet 43.5 percent of India's rural poor are concentrated in these groups. Poverty rates among scheduled castes and tribe households are significantly higher than the rest of the population- in 1993-94 the proportion of rural SC and ST households below poverty line were 49.0 and 49.5 percent respectively as compared to a poverty rate of 32.8 percent for rural non-scheduled households. From above table we see a gap in the proportion living in poverty (a poverty rate gap) of 16.2 percent (49.0-32.8) between SC and nonscheduled households., and a poverty rate gap of 16.7 percent (=49.5-32.8) between ST and nonscheduled households. One major task in the in the fight to reduce rural poverty is to close the gap in poverty rates between scheduled caste and tribes and non-scheduled group.

Labor Force Participation Rate (LFR), Worker Population Rate (WPR) and Unemployment Rate (UR) according to usual status for persons of age 15 years and above in Rural sector were as follows

Table 12

· Labor Force Participation Rate

YEAR	WFR			LFPR			UR		
	Male	Female	Total	Male	Female	Total	Male	Female	Total
2017-18	72.0	23.7	48.1	76.4	24.6	50.7	5.7	3.8	5.3
2018-19	72.2	25.5	48.9	76.4	26.4	51.5	5.5	3.5	5.0
2019-20	74.4	32.2	53.3	77.9	33.0	55.5	4.5	2.6	3.9
2020-21	75.1	35.8	55.5	78.1	36.5	57.4	3.8	2.1	3.3
2021-22	75.3	35.8	55.6	78.2	36.6	57.5	3.8	2.1	3.2

• **Source: Periodic Labor Force Survey Report; Government of India.**

The bulk of India's poor live in rural areas. However, the rural-urban distribution of the poor has declined, from 81.33% in rural and 18,67% in urban areas in 1973-74 to 73.2% in rural and 26.8% in urban areas in 2004-05 (Table 8). It is obvious that in rural areas, the percentage of persons making some tangible effort to get employment for about one year or less is 48.65 of the unemployed persons. Whereas the number of persons seeking for more than one year constitute the number of persons seeking for more than one year constitute 51.35 percent. In the urban areas of the State 56.32 per cent of the total unemployed persons were found to be seeking or available for work for more than one year, as compared to 45.53 per cent for all India. This proportion was 58.86 percent in Kerala, 56.91 per cent in Tamil Nadu, 53.15 per cent in Andhra Pradesh and 43.51 percent in Maharashtra.

Table 13

- **Poverty Rate**

	SCHEDULED CASTE	SCHEDULED TRIBE	NON SCHEDULED	ALL
Overall	49	49.5	32.8	38.3
AGE				
20-29	45.3	48.6	30.2	36.5
30-39	55.9	56.6	38.2	44.7
40-49	48.9	48.2	32.1	37.6
50-59	43.9	43.0	29.8	34.2
60-70	44.3	43.4	30.0	34.1
HOUSEHOLD SIZE				
1	21.5	11.3	14.7	16.0
2	28.9	24.8	16.7	20.9
3	36.0	39.1	23.5	28.4
4	49.3	49.5	27.5	35.2
5	54.1	54.5	36.2	42.3
6	59.3	61.6	42.2	48.2
7 or more	65.2	64.3	44.0	50.0
EDUCATION				
Not Literate	53.6	54.0	40.6	46.1

Literate, below Primary	44.5	43.8	32.5	36.9
Literate, below secondary	38.4	40.6	27.2	30.0
Literate, Secondary	32.8	25.3	16.3	18.7
Literate, higher secondary & above	23.3	14.9	9.9	11.6
OCCUPATION				
Self-employed in non-agricultural	41.9	40.8	30.1	32.9
Self-employed in agricultural	37.4	44.9	26.5	29.9
Agricultural labor	58.6	58.3	50.8	54.7
Non-agricultural labor	45.0	52.6	37.3	41.7
Others	23.3	22.6	19.4	20.2

- **Sources: 50ʰ Round (1993-94) Of the consumer expenditure Survey of the N S S.**

Growing population has forward and backward linkages with the other economic dynamics particularly poverty and unemployment. Raising population is accompanied by a rise in the labor force of the community which leads the substantial chunk of population to unemployment. The rising population has serious implications on poverty also.

Table 14

Rural-Urban distribution of the poor, 1973-74 to 2004-05

YEAR	TOTAL POPULATION BELOW POVERTY LINE (MILLION)			PERCENT OF INDIA'S POOR	
	INDIA	RURAL	URBAN	RURAL	URBAN
1973-74	321.3	261.3	60.0	81.33	18.67
1977-78	328.9	264.3	64.6	80.36	19.64
1983	322.9	252.0	70.9	78.04	21.96
1987-88	307.1	231.9	75.2	75.51	24.49
1993-94	320.3	244.0	76.3	76.18	23.82
1999-00	260.2*	193.2*	67.0*	74.30	25.70
2004-05	301.7	220.9	80.8	73.20	26.80

- **Note:* estimates for 1999-00 are based on the mrp method and not comparable with estimates for other years, which are based on the upr method.**

- Source: Planning Commission (1997), Press Information Bureau (2001, 2007).

The bulk of India's poor live in rural areas. However, the rural-urban distribution of the poor has declined, from 81.33% in rural and 18.67% in urban areas in 1973-74 to 73.2% in rural and 26.8% in urban areas in 2004-05 (Table 14). Even though rural-urban differences in poverty incidence were recognized from the start in assessing the extent of poverty in the country, a 1996 report provided a comprehensive assessment of poverty incidence. Before we turn to reporting the poverty estimates, we should clarify that while we have defended the current poverty line in India for both purposes-tracking abject poverty and redistribution- in general, we believe a case exists for two separate poverty lines to satisfy the two objectives.

The tribal population of the country, as per 2011 census, is 104.3 million, constituting 8.6% of the total population, 89.9% of them live in rural areas and 10.03% in urban areas. The decadal population growth of the tribal from Census 2001 to 2011 has been 23.66% against the 17.69% of the entire population. The sex ratio for the overall population is 940females per 1000 males and that of Scheduled Tribes 990 females per

1000 males. The trends in ST population since Census 1961 is illustrated in Table-12. From 30.1 million in 1961, the ST population has increased to 104.3 million in 2011.

Table 15

· Trends in Proportion of Scheduled Tribe Population

TRENDS IN PROPORTION OF ST POPULATION			
CENSUS YEAR	TOTAL POPULATION (IN MILLION)	SCHEDULED TRIBES POPULATION (IN MILLION)	PROPORTION OF ST POPULATION
1961	439.2	30.1	6.9
1971	547.9	38.0	6.9
1981*	665.3	51.6	7.8
1991**	838.6	67.8	8.1
2001***	1028.6	84.3	8.2
2011	1210.8	104.3	8.6

- Excludes Assam in 1981

- ** Excludes Jammu & Kashmir in 1991.

- *** The figures exclude This excludes some parts of Manipur in 2001.

The Scheduled Castes and Scheduled Tribes comprise about 16.6% and 8.6%, respectively, of India's population (according to the 2011 census). The *Constitution (Scheduled Castes) Order, 1950* lists 1,108 castes across 28 states in its First Schedule, and the *Constitution (Scheduled Tribes) Order, 1950* lists 744 tribes. Broadly the ST's inhabit two distinct geographical areas– the Central India and the Northeastern Areas.

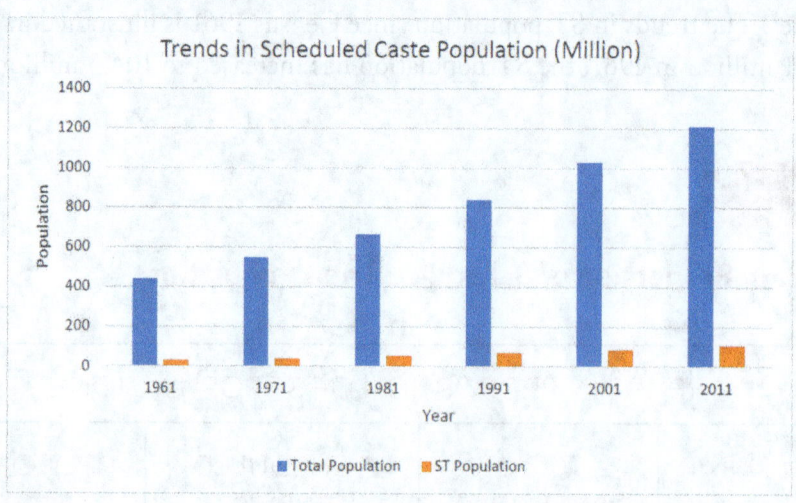

Trends in Scheduled Caste Population (Million)

CHAPTER IV

AN OVERVIEW OF POVERTY BY CASTE:

The Scheduled Caste constitutes a significant demographic strength in India. Most of India's poor live in rural areas. Our focus is on rural poverty. Most of India's poor live in rural areas. The Caste based ideology of hereditary occupations prescribes the most minimal and lowly of occupations to SC groups and has determined the socio-economic life of these communities. While SC's have traditionally been denied education, even those with education have experienced very limited social mobility due to caste-based opposition to their occupational mobility (Jefferey et., al. 2002). On the other hand, the Scheduled Tribes belong to different set of economic and cultural factors that have little to do with caste ideology. Scheduled Tribes has isolated from mainstream of Indian society. This has afforded them a measure of cultural autonomy and economic independence. Modernization and accumulative processes of production have resulted in massive encroachment into their natural habits. This has intern resulted in displacement, poverty and heightened levels of exploitation through a system of 'boded labor'. The histories of exploitation and marginalization of Scheduled Caste and Scheduled Tribe communities have produced different engagements with education as a path to social mobility.

Recent studies show that there is an increased demand for education among Scheduled Caste and Scheduled Tribes (M Sedwal, 2008). A little over 73 percent of the households belonged to rural India and accounted for nearly 75 percent of total population. About 9 percent of the households in the country belonged to *scheduled tribes* (ST), about 20 percent belonged to *scheduled caste* (SC) and about 40 percent belonged to the *other backward class* (OBC). About 8 percent, 20 percent and 41 percent of the Indian population belonged to the categories ST, SC, and OBC. The proportion of persons belonging to the categories ST, SC and OBC were about 11 percent, 22 percent and 42 percent, respectively in the rural areas and about 3 percent, 15 percent and 36 percent, respectively in the urban areas.

Table 16

Literacy Rates for Total and Backward Caste by Sex- 2001

STATES/UT	PROPORTION OF SC &ST POPULATION		LITERACY RATE OF SC &ST POPULATION
	SC	ST	SC
INDIA	16.2	8.2	54.69
Jammu & Kashmir	7.6	10.9	59.03
Himachal Pradesh	24.7	4.0	70.31
Punjab	28.9	-	56.22
Chandigarh	17.5	-	67.66
Uttaranchal	17.9	3.0	63.40
Haryana	19.3	-	55.45
Delhi	16.9	-	70.85
Rajasthan	17.2	12.6	52.24
Uttar Pradesh	21.1	0.1	46.27
Bihar	15.7	0.9	28.47
Sikkim	5.0	20.6	63.04
Arunachal Pradesh	0.6	64.2	67.64
Nagaland	-	89.1	-
Manipur	2.8	34.2	72.32
Mizoram	-	94.5	89.20
Tripura	17.4	31.1	74.68

Meghalaya	0.5	85.9	56.27
Assam	6.9	12.4	66.78
West Bengal	23.0	5.5	59.04
Jharkhand	11.8	26.3	37.56
Orissa	16.5	22.1	55.53
Chhattisgarh	11.6	31.8	63.96
Madhya Pradesh	15.2	20.3	58.57
Gujarat	7.1	14.8	70.50
Daman & Diu	3.1	8.8	85.13
Dadar & Nagar Haveli	1.9	62.2	78.25
Maharashtra	10.2	8.9	71.90
Andhra Pradesh	16.2	6.6	53.52
Karnataka	16.2	6.6	52.87
Gao	1.8	-	71.92
Lakshadweep	-	94.5	-
Kerala	9.8	1.1	82.66
Tamil Nadu	19.0	1.0	63.19
Pondicherry	16.2	0.0	69.12
Andaman & Nicobar Island	0.0	8.3	-

• *Source: Government of India (2006)*

According to the 2001 census, the ST population is 84,326,240 and constitutes 8.2 percent of the total population of India. This population grew by 24.5% during the period 1991-2001 (Census of India, 2002). The SC population on the other hand, is 166,635,700 and constitutes 16.2 percent of the total population of India. The cultural marginalization and oppression faced by Scheduled Caste and Scheduled Tribes that mainstream education is its inability to deliver the promise of jobs and upward economic mobility. In the experience of Scheduled Caste and Scheduled Tribes, therefore, failure to get a job in the modern economy means a double loss, because the 'educated' child is ill equipped and/or unwilling to participate in the economic activity of the household. The reluctance of SC and ST parents to keep their children in school can be traced to the disconnection between school education and their prospects in the economy. The discontent with schooling as a path towards social and economic mobility is only likely to increase among Scheduled Caste and Scheduled Tribes with the growth in the casualization of the labor force in urban and rural sector, a phenomenon that started in the 1990's with economic liberalization reforms.

We thus see that the child sex ratio patterns among the scheduled castes have tended to follow the pattern among the 'general' or the other castes rather than those among the scheduled tribes. Thus, clubbing the two groups together, as is traditionally done in the policy as well as academic circles is inappropriate. Second, the role of the 'region' seems to be more significant than the factor of being the part of 'Scheduled Castes'. An interesting statistic on the f/m ratio among the 0-4 and 5-9 age group by the percent of the SC population in three group of districts with low (<10%), medium (10-20%) and high (>20%) percentage of the SC population. Among districts with low, moderate and high concentration of the Scheduled caste population one could notice lowering of FMR 5-9 among the districts where scheduled caste population has moderate or high concentration. A further indication perhaps that in such districts the scheduled tribes.

We thus see that the child sex ratio patterns among the scheduled castes have tended to castes start behaving 'more like the higher castes than they used to be' as described by Dreze and Sen (1995) for the SC population in UP. Goody and Berreman in their persuasive analyses have already drawn attention towards female subordination being a 'precondition' of upward social mobility a point further amplified by Vishwanath (2004) more recently in the context of the analysis of the female infanticide during the colonial rule. As long, as the scheduled castes follow the same female-regressive social make up that has characterized the landowning and hypergamous upper castes, the cancer of female feticide is bound to spread among them. Given the process of 'Sanskritization' they are subject to this is inevitable unless social reform accompanies their upward mobility. Higher female workforce participation which had earlier characterized the scheduled castes may come down in the wake of prosperity for the sake of 'status production' (Papanek, 1989). The SC female children may then face the double burden; Sanskritization on one hand and reduced economic worth on the other. Extricating them from the 'twin danger' is a challenge for the society indeed scheduled tribes. Thus, clubbing the two groups together, as is traditionally done in the policy as well as academic circles is inappropriate. Second, the role of the 'region' seems to be more significant than the factor of being the part of 'scheduled castes.

During 2004-2005, the household size in the rural areas was the lowest among the ST's (4.6). In the urban areas, it was lowest for both ST's and others (4.3) each. During the same period, the overall sex ratio in India was 951 females per 1000 males. The sex ratio was 959 among the ST's 954 for both the SC's and OBC's, and 943 among others. In rural India, proportion of households depending on self-employment was higher among the other category of households (61 percent) or among OBC category of households (56 percent) as compared to that among the ST (46 precent) or SC (34 percent) households. In urban India too, proportion of households depending on self-employment was higher among the OBC households (40 percent) and others category in 2004-2005, the household size in the rural areas was the lowest among the ST's (4.6). In the urban areas, it was lowest for both in 2004-2005, the household size in the rural areas was the lowest among the ST's (4.6). In the urban areas, it was lowest for both2004-2005, the household size in the rural areas was the lowest among the ST's (4.6). In the urban areas, it was lowest for both ST's and others (4.3) each.

During the same period, the overall sex ratio in India was 951 females per 1000 males. The sex ratio was 959 among the ST's 954 for both the SC's and OBC's, and 943 among 20042005, the household size in the rural areas was the lowest among the ST's (4.6). In the urban areas, it was lowest for both ST's and others (4.3) each. During the same period, the overall sex ratio in India was 951 females per 1000 males. The sex ratio was 959 among the ST's 954 for both the SC's and OBC's, and 943 among others. In rural India, proportion of households depending on self-employment was higher among the other category of households (61 percent) or others. In rural India, proportion of households depending on self-employment was higher among the other category of households (61 percent) or ST's and others (4.3) each. During the same period, the overall sex ratio in India was 951 females per 1000 males. The sex ratio was 959 among the ST's 954 for both the SC's and OBC's, and 943 among others.

In rural India, proportion of households depending on self-employment was higher among the other category of households (61 percent) or ST's and others (4.3) each. During the same period, the overall sex ratio in India was 951 females per 1000 males. The sex ratio was 959 among the ST's 954 for both the SC's and OBC's, and 943 among others. In rural India, proportion of households depending on self-employment was higher among the other category of households (61 percent) or households (39 precent) as compared to that among the ST (26 percent) or SC (29 percent) households. In the rural areas, the proportion of households in the higst monthly per-capita consumer expenditure (MPCE) class (i.e., those who spent Rs. 1155 or more per month) was higher among other categories of households (12 percent) than among the OBC's (5 percent), SC's (3 percent) or ST's (2 percent). The proportion of urban households in the highest MPCE class (I.e., those who spent Rs. 2540 or more per month) was higher among other (13 percent) category of households than among the OBC's or ST's (3 percent each) or SC's (1 percent).

About 26 percent of the households in the rural areas and 8 percent in the urban areas had no literate members of age 15 years and above. The proportion of households without any literate adult (15 years and above) member or without any literate adult female member was much higher among the households belonging to the ST's and SCs compared to the OBC's or other category households in both rural and urban India. In the rural areas, for every 1000 households, about 17 households reported that at least one male member had got the work in public works, whereas only 8 households reported that at least one female member had got the work in public works for at least 60 days during the previous 365 days. Among the social groups, the incidence is found to be higher for the ST's followed by the SC's and OBC's.

About 34 percent people of India were literate. The literacy rate was the highest among the others (78 percent) category of people, followed by the OBC's with a gap of nearly 13 percentage points, and the lowest among the ST's (52 percent). According to the usual status, about 56 percent of rural males and 33 percent of rural females belonged to the labor force. The corresponding proportions in the urban areas were 57 percent and 18 percent, respectively. According to the usual status, about 42 percent of the population in the country was usually employed. The proportion was 44 percent in the rural and 37 percent in the urban. About 55 percent of rural males and 33 percent of rural female were employed. The corresponding proportion in the urban areas were 55 percent and 17 percent, respectively. The Worker Proportion Ratio (WPR) according to the usual status, was the highest among the males (56 percent) and females (44 percent) belonging to the ST's (50 percent). In urban India, however, the proportion of person employed was the same among SC and ST workers (38 percent each) and was about 35 percent among others. Among the rural males WPR was higher for persons belonging to ST's (89 percent) and SC's (86 percent) than that for OBC's (85 percent) and other (82 percent).

In the rural areas, among both males and females, the proportion of chronically unemployed was the highest for the other category of persons. Between the two categories of ST's and SC's rural households, proportion of chronically unemployed among the males and females was higher among the SC's than among the ST's. Among the urban males, the proportion of chronically unemployed was the highest among SC's followed by that among the other categories. For urban females, the proportion of chronically unemployed was slightly lower for SC's and ST's than for those belong to the OBC's or another category.

When we look poverty at the State and National Level, the most wonderful fact is that the poverty ratio of these States which participated the most in the economic reform process such as Maharashtra, Tamil Nadu, Karnataka, Madhya Pradesh, West Bengal have more poverty ratio than that States which participated least such as Kerala, Punjab, Haryana, Rajasthan, etc. So, it is evident that no certain and positive relationship between economic reform and poverty elimination. As far as the matter of poverty reduction is concerned, the poor people have to be provided meaningful employment and the availability of essential goods for their lives and lively hood.

Table 17

· POVERTY RATIO OF DIFFERENT STATES OF INDIA

STATES/ YEAR	1987-1988		1993-1994		1999-2000
	RURAL	URBAN	RURAL	URBAN	RURAL
Jammu & Kashmir	25.70	17.47	30.34	9.18	3.97
Punjab	12.60	14.67	11.95	11.35	6.35
Himachal Pradesh	16.28	6.29	30.34	9.18	7.94
Haryana	16.22	17.99	28.02	16.38	8.27
Kerala	29.10	40.33	25.76	24.55	9.38
Gujarat	28.67	37.26	22.18	27.89	13.17
Rajasthan	33.21	41.92	26.46	30.49	13.74
Andhra Pradesh	20.92	40.11	15.92	38.33	10.05
Mizoram	39.35	9.94	45.01	7.73	40.04
Karnataka	32.89	48.12	29.88	40.14	17.38

Tamil Nadu	45.80	38.64	32.48	22.14	20.55
Maharashtra	40.78	39.78	37.93	35.15	23.72
West Bengal	48.30	35.08	40.80	22.41	31.85
Manipur	39.35	9.94	45.01	7.73	40.04
Uttar Pradesh	14.10	42.96	42.28	35.59	31.22
Nagaland	39.35	9.94	45.01	7.73	40.04
Arunachal Pradesh	39.35	9.94	45.01	7.73	40.04
Meghalaya	39.35	9.94	45.01	7.73	40.04
Tripura	39.35	9.94	45.01	7.73	40.04
Assam	39.35	9.94	45.01	7.73	40.04
Sikkim	39.34	9.94	45.01	7.73	40.04
Madhya Pradesh	41.92	47.09	40.64	48.38	37.06
Bihar	52.63	48.73	58.21	34.50	44.30
Orissa	57.64	41.63	49.72	41.64	48.01
All India	39.09	38.20	37.27	32.36	27.09

• **Source: Planning Commission, Five-year plan (2002-2007), Govt. of India.**

Poverty is essentially a problem of low/ almost nil productivity of the poor. These people either do not produce or produce very little, so that their income remains low for a level of consumption- experience can lift them above their miserable living. The problem of poverty and unemployment is considered as a biggest challenge to development planning in India. High poverty level is synonymous with poor quality of life. About 320 million people of India live below poverty line in 1993-94. This constitutes as much as 35.97% of the total population of the country. The poor in the rural areas are 37.27% of the rural population. Those in the urban areas account for 32.36% of the urban population. Unemployment simply means a situation when able and willing people are not getting jobs as per their own capabilities. Unemployment in India is structural in nature, i.e., productive capacity is inadequate to create enough jobs. This is a chronic phenomenon.It is true that economic growth creates opportunities for employment. Rural unemployed were ignored in comparison with urban unemployed persons. As a result, rural unemployed are running towards the urban areas. If this acute problem of unemployment is not solved, then there will be an explosive situation in future.

Table 18

· PAST AND PRESENT EMPLOYMENT AND UNEMPLOYMENT SCENARIO

	MILLION			GROWTH PER ANNUM
	1983	1993-1994	1999-2000	1993-1994
ALL INDIA				
Population	718.20	894.01	1003.93	2.00
Labor Force	261.33	335.97	363.33	2.43
Unemployment Rate (%)	(8.30)	(5.99)	(7.32)	-
No. of unemployed	21.76	20.13	26.38	-0.08
RURAL				
Population	546.61	658.83	727.50	1.79
Labor Force	204.18	255.38	270.89	2.15
Workforce	187.92	241.04	250.89	2.40
Unemployment Rate (%)	(7.96)	(5.61)	(7.21)	

No. Of unemployed	16.26	14.34	19.50	-1.19
URBAN				
Population	171.59	234.98	276.47	3.04
Labor Force	57.15	89.60	92.95	3.33
Workforce	51.64	74.80	85.84	3.59

• Source: Planning Commission.

As the economic reform took place in India, the number of forces causing unemployment increased and thus increasing, the number of poor and hence the problem of poverty. Unemploy-ment is the outcome of this gigantic development and poverty is the progeny of progress. About 260.2 million people in India, living below the poverty line. The availability of detailed infor-mation vis a vis the earlier estimates, from 1972-73 (NSSO Surveys) changed the official approach to employment in mid-1970's. It was increasingly realized that economic growth alone could not be relied upon to tackle the issue of unemployment anymore. Therefore, a number of employment generation and unemployment rates over NSS rounds is given below.

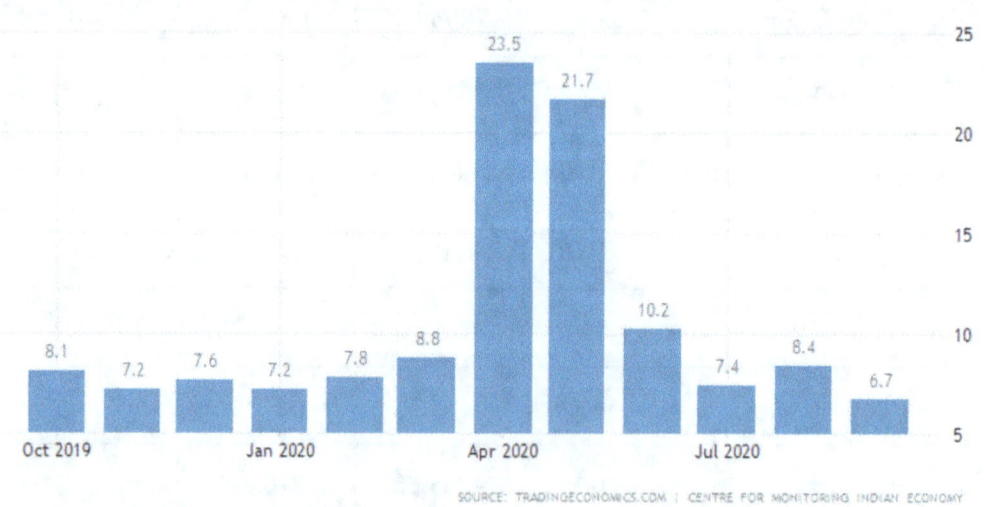

• **India's Unemployment Rate**

Table 19

- ## Unemployment rates (per 1000 persons in labor force) all-India

ROUNDS (YEAR)	UNEMPLOYMENT RATES							
	MALE				FEMALE			
	Usual status (ps)	Usual Status (adj)	CWS	CDS	Usual status (ps)	Usual status (adj)	CWS	CDS
RURAL								
68th 2011-12	21	17	33	55	29	17	35	62
66th 2009-10	19	16	32	64	24	16	37	80
61th 2004-05	21	16	38	80	31	18	42	87
55th 1999-00	21	17	39	72	15	10	37	70
50th 1993-94	20	14	31	56	13	9	29	56
43rd 1987-88	28	18	42	46	35	24	44	67
38th 1983	21	14	37	75	14	7	43	90
32nd 1977-78	22	13	36	71	55	20	41	92
27th 1972-73	-	12	30	68	-	5	55	112
URBAN								
68th 2011-12	32	30	38	49	66	52	67	80
66th 2009-10	30	28	36	51	70	57	72	91
61th 2004-05	44	38	52	75	91	69	90	116
55th 1999-00	48	45	56	73	71	57	73	94

50ᵗʰ1993-94	54	41	52	67	83	61	79	104
43ʳᵈ1987-88	61	52	66	88	85	62	92	120
38ᵗʰ1983	59	51	67	92	69	49	75	110
32ⁿᵈ1977-78	65	54	71	94	178	124	109	145
27ᵗʰ1972-73	-	48	60	80	-	60	92	137

The availability of detailed information vis a vis the earlier estimates, from 1972-73 (NSSO) changed the official approach to employment in mid1970's. It was increasingly realized that economic growth alone could not be relied upon to tackle the poverty alleviation programs that were started since fifth five-year plan (1974-79). The summary of unemployment rates over NSS rounds is given in Table 13. While employment growth has been lowering in 2009-10 and 2011-12, unemployment rate in India continued to hover around 2 percent under usual status (ps+ss) and fell under CDS (current daily status). Although the unemployment rate may be lower than what is prevailing now in developed economics, the number of unemployed people was 11.3 million, which declined to 9.8 million in 2009-10 but again increased to 10.8 million in 2011-12 under usual status (ps + ss). However, based on the CDS the number of unemployed person days declined from 34.3 million in 2004-05 to 28.0 million in 2009-10 and further to 24.7 million in 2011-12. Thus, there is steep reduction in unemployment rate under CDS from 8.2 percent in 2004-05 to 5.6 percent in 2011-12.

Overall, unemployment rate were lower in 2009-10 under each approach vis-à-vis 200405 and during 2011-12 compared to 2009-10, as per UPS (adj) approach, it remained invariant for rural males (2 percent), rural females (2 percent) and urban males (3 percent) but decreased by 1 percentage point for urban females (from 6 percent in 2009-10 to 5 percent in 2011-12). The fall in unemployment despite marginal growth in employment in 2009-10 (1.1 million jobs created PS+SS, 2004-05 to 2009-10) and 2011-12 (13.9 million jobs created PS+SS, 1999-2000 to 200405) could also be on account of the demographic dividend, as an increasing proportion of the young population opts for education rather than participating in the labor market. This is reflected in the rise in growth in enrolment of students in higher education from 4.9 million in 1990-91 to 28.5 million in 2011-12.

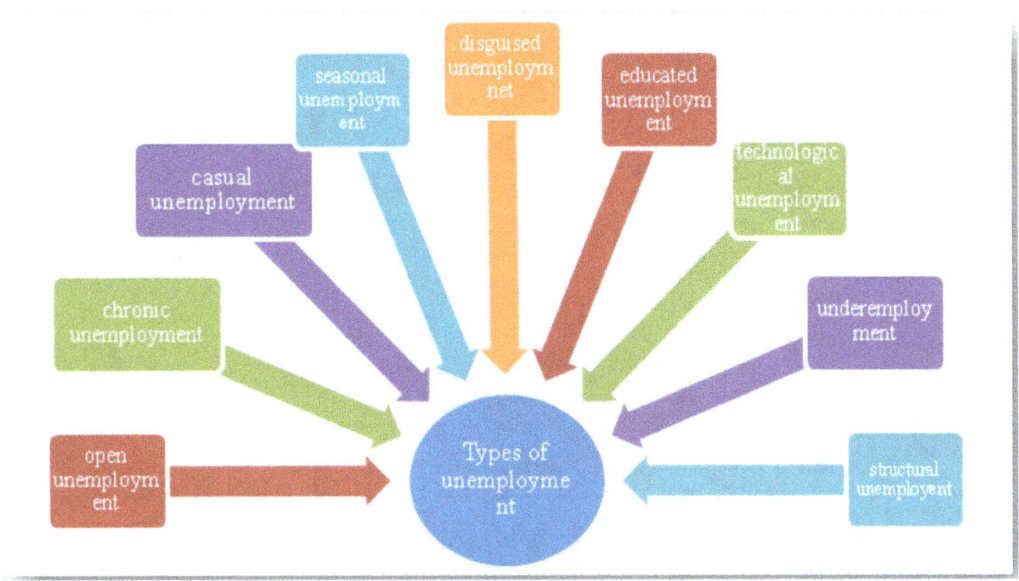

According to the 2001 Census of India, scheduled castes and tribes comprise 16.2 percent and 8.2 percent, respectively, of India's population, yet 47.3 percent of India's rural poor are concentrated in these groups.[7] The incidence of poverty among scheduled caste and tribe households is much higher than for the rest of the population—in 1999/2000 the proportion of rural SC and ST households below the poverty line were 30.1 and 39.4 percent respectively, as compared with a poverty rate of 17.7 percent for rural non-scheduled households. From Table we see a gap in the proportion living in poverty (a poverty incidence gap) of 12.4 percent (= 30.1- 17.7) between SC and non-scheduled households, and a poverty incidence gap of 21.7 percent (= 39.4- 17.7) between ST and non-scheduled households.

We study the causes of higher poverty amongst SC and ST households compared with nonscheduled households. We ask whether differences in the amounts of schooling, occupational choice and demographic characteristics hold the key to understanding the poverty incidence gap, and whether the poverty mitigating strength of household or individual characteristics (e.g. education and occupation) are different for each group. To answer these questions, we first examine the determinants of poverty for scheduled

---

[7] These estimates are from the unit record data provided in the National Sample Survey's 55th round of the consumer expenditure survey. More details of the computations are provided in the next section. These calculations used the official poverty lines from the Indian Planning Commission. Using alternative Deaton–Tarozzi (DT) poverty lines, available for a subset of States and Union Territories, scheduled groups com¬prise 48.6 percent of India's rural poor. We discuss the choice of poverty lines below.

households, SC and ST, and non-scheduled households, and implement an Oaxaca-type decomposition methodology that allows us to examine causes of the disparity in poverty incidence.

Table 20

· State Wise Population of Scheduled caste and Scheduled Tribes 2011

SL NO	STATES/UT	PERCENT OF SC POPULATION	PERCENT OF ST POPULATION	PERCENT OF OBC
1	Andhra Pradesh	16.41	7.00	50.4
2	Arunachal Pradesh	0.00	68.79	2.8
3	Assam	7.15	12.45	25.3
4	Bihar	15.91	1.28	62.6
5	Chhattisgarh	12.82	30.62	45.5
6	Goa	1.74	10,23	17.9
7	Gujrat	6.74	14.75	40.2
8	Haryana	20.17	0.00	28.3
9	Himachal Pradesh	25.19	5.71	17.1
10	Jammu & Kashmir	7.38	11.91	11.4
11	Jharkhand	12.08	26.21	46.8
12	Karnataka	17.15	6.95	55.5
13	Kerala	9.10	1.45	65.3
14	Madhya Pradesh	15.62	21.09	41.3
15	Maharashtra	11.81	9.35	33.8

16	Manipur	3.41	40.88	52.7
17	Meghalaya	0.58	86.15	1.2
18	Mizoram	0.11	94.43	1.6
19	Nagaland	0.00	86.48	0.2
20	Orissa	17.13	22.85	33.2
21	Punjab	31.94	0.00	16.1
22	Rajasthan	17.83	13.48	47.3
23	Sikkim	4.63	33.80	50.6
24	Tamil Nadu	20.01	1.10	76.1
25	Tripura	17.83	31.76	16.4
26	Uttar Pradesh	20.70	0.57	54.3
27	Uttarakhand	18.76	2.89	18.3
28	West Bengal	23.51	5.80	8.7
29	A & N Island	0.00	7.50	18.1
30	Chandigarh	18,86	0.00	22.2
31	D & N Haveli	1.80	51.95	4.3
32	Daman & Diu	2.52	6.32	37.9
33	NCT of Delhi	16.75	0.00	19.5
34	Puducherry	15.73	0.00	77.1
	INDIA	16.63	8.63	44..0

• Source; Census of India

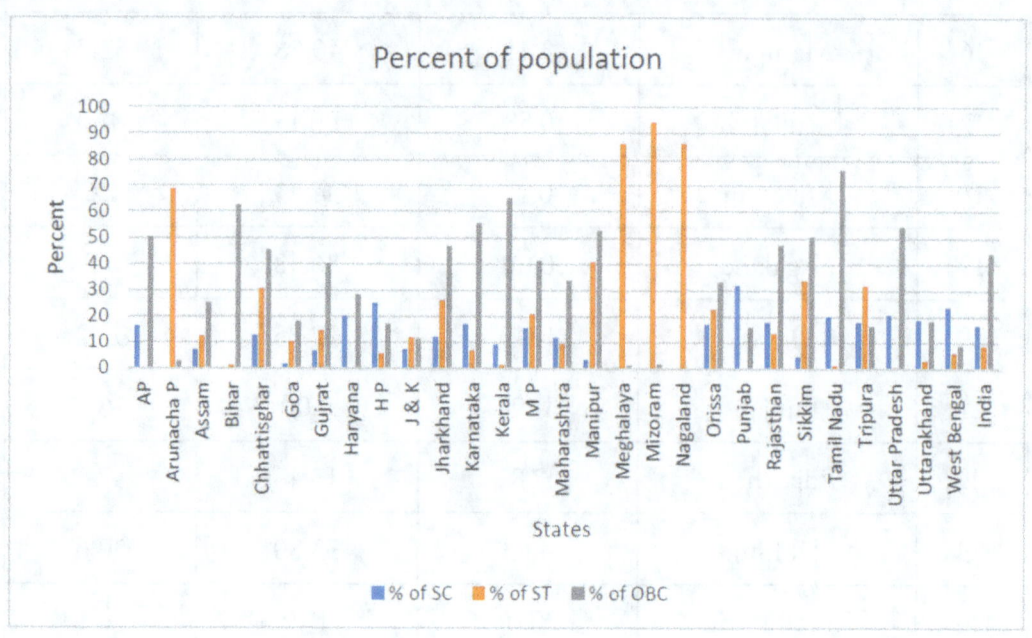

We use rural household survey data on 67,942 households from the 55th round of the National Sample Survey (NSS). We estimate regression equations where the dependent variable is the natural logarithm of the ratio of (monthly) per capita expenditure to the poverty line, following an approach suggested in Coudouel *et al.* (2002), later referred to as the World Bank approach. The likelihood of being in poverty can be calculated using the standard normal distribution function and transforming the regression coefficients by dividing them with the standard deviation of the error term. Based on this calculation of the likelihood of being in poverty for scheduled and nonscheduled groups, we can construct a decomposition equation that explains differences in the incidence of poverty in terms of differences in characteristics (characteristics effect) and differences in the "transformed regression" coefficients (coefficients effect).

CHAPTER V

LABOR AND EMPLOYMENT

Thus, there is steep reduction only a tiny fraction of India's surface area is uninhabited. More than half of it is cultivated, with little left fallow in any given year. Most of the area classified as forest—roughly one-fifth of the total—is used for grazing, for gathering firewood and other forest products, for commercial forestry, and, in tribal areas, for shifting cultivation (often in defiance of the law) and hunting. The areas too dry for growing crops without irrigation are largely used for grazing. The higher elevations of the Himalayas are the only places with substantial continuous areas not in use by humans. Although India's population is predominantly rural, the country has three of the largest urban areas in the world—Mumbai, Kolkata (Calcutta), and Delhi— and those and other large Indian cities have some of the world's highest population densities.

• **Hoshiarpur, Punjab, India: communal well**

Communal well, Hoshiarpur, Punjab, India.

Shostal Associates

Most Indians reside in the areas of continuous cultivation, including the towns and cities they encompass. Within such areas, differences in population density are largely a function of water availability (whether directly from rainfall or from irrigation) and soil fertility. Areas receiving more than 60 inches (1,500 mm) of annual precipitation are generally capable of, for example, growing two crops per year, even without irrigation, and thus can support a high population density. More than three-fifths of the total population lives either on the fertile alluvial soils of the <u>Indo-Gangetic Plain</u> and the deltaic regions of the eastern coast or on the mixed alluvial and marine soils along India's western coast. Within those agriculturally productive areas—for example, parts of the eastern Gangetic Plain and of the state of Kerala—densities exceed 2,000 persons per square mile (800 persons per square km).

Much of India's rural population lives in nucleated <u>villages</u>, which most commonly have a settlement form described as a shapeless agglomerate. Such settlements, though unplanned, are divided by caste into distinct wards and grow outward from a recognizable core area. The dominant and higher castes tend to live in the core area, while the lower artisan and service castes, as well as Muslim groups, generally occupy more peripheral localities. When the centrally located castes increase in population, they either subdivide their existing, often initially large, residential compounds, add second and even third stories on their existing houses (a common expedient in Punjab), leapfrog over lower-caste wards to a new area on the village periphery, or, in rare cases where land is available, found a completely new village.

Within the shapeless agglomerated villages, streets are typically narrow, twisting, and unpaved, often ending in culs-de-sac. There are usually a few open spaces where people gather: adjacent to a temple or mosque, at the main village well, in areas where grain is threshed or where grain and oilseeds are milled, and in front of the homes of the leading families of the village. In such spaces, depending on the size of the village, might be found the *panchayat* (village council) hall, a few shops, a tea stall, a public radio hooked up to a loudspeaker, a small post office, or perhaps a *dharmshala* (a free guest house for travelers). The village school is usually on the edge of the village in order to provide pupils with adequate playing space.

Much of India's rural population lives in nucleated villages, which most commonly have a settlement form described as a shapeless agglomerate. Such settlements, though unplanned, are divided by caste into distinct wards and grow outward from a recognizable core area. The dominant and higher castes tend to live in the core area, while the lower artisan and service castes, as well as Muslim groups, generally occupy more peripheral localities. When the centrally located castes increase in population, they either subdivide their existing, often initially large, residential compounds, add second and even third stories on their existing houses (a common expedient in Punjab), leapfrog over lower-caste wards to a new area on the village periphery, or, in rare cases where land is available, found a completely new village.

Within the shapeless agglomerated villages, streets are typically narrow, twisting, and unpaved, often ending in culs-de-sac. There are usually a few open spaces where people gather: adjacent to a temple or mosque, at the main village well, in areas where grain is threshed or where grain and oilseeds are milled, and in front of the homes of the leading families of the village. In such spaces, depending on the size of the village, might be found the *panchayat* (village council) hall, a few shops, a tea stall, a public radio hooked up to a loudspeaker, a small post office, or perhaps a *dharmshala* (a free guest house for travelers). The village school is usually on the edge of the village in order to provide pupils with adequate playing space. Another common feature along the margin of a village is a grove of mango or other trees, which provides shade for people and animals and often contains a large well.

Time-lapse video of Madurai, a city in the southern Indian state of Tamil Nadu, featuring the shrines and pillared halls of the Hindu Meenakshi Amman (Minakshi-Sundareshwara) Temple. There are many regional variants from the simple agglomerated villages pattern. Hamlets, each containing only one or a few castes, commonly surround villages in the eastern Gangetic Plain; Scheduled Castes and herding castes are likely to occupy such hamlets. In southern India, especially Tamil Nadu, and in Gujarat, villages have a more planned layout, with streets running northsouth and east-west in straight lines. In many tribal areas (or areas that were tribal until relatively recently) the typical village consists of rows of houses along a single street or perhaps two or three parallel streets. In areas of rugged terrain, where relatively level spaces for building are limited, settlements often conform in shape to ridge lines, and few grow to be larger than hamlets. Finally, in particularly aquatic environments, such as the Gangetic delta region and the tidal backwater region of Kerala, agglomerations of even hamlet size are rare; most rural families instead live singly or in clusters of only a few households on their individual plots of owned or rented land.

Most village houses are small, simple one-story mud (*kacha*) structures, housing both people and livestock in one or just a few rooms. Roofs typically are flat and made of mud in dry regions, but in areas with considerable precipitation they generally are sloped for drainage and made of rice straw, other thatching material, or clay tiles. The wetter the region, the greater the pitch of the roof. In some wet regions, especially in tribal areas, bamboo walls are more common than those of mud, and houses often stand on piles above ground level. The houses usually are windowless and contain a minimum of furniture, a storage space for food, water, and implements, a few shelves and pegs for other possessions, a niche in the wall to serve as the household altar, and often a few decorations, such as pictures of gods or film heroes, family photographs, a calendar, or perhaps some memento of a pilgrimage. In one corner of the house or in an exterior court is the earthen hearth on which all meals are cooked. Electricity, running water, and toilet facilities generally are absent. Relatively secluded spots on the edge of the village serve the latter need.

Almost everywhere in India, the dwellings of the more affluent households are larger and usually built of more durable (*pakka*) materials, such as brick or stone. Their roofs are also of sturdier construction, sometimes of corrugated iron, and often rest on sturdy timbers or even steel beams. Windows, usually barred for security, are common. The number of rooms, the furnishings, and the interior and exterior decor, especially the entrance gate, generally reflect the wealth of the family. There is typically an interior compound where much of the harvest will be stored. Within the compound there may be a private well or even a hand pump, an area for bathing, and a walled latrine enclosure, which is periodically cleaned by the village sweeper. Animal stalls, granaries, and farm equipment are in spaces distinct from those occupied by people.

Nomadic groups may be found in most parts of India. Some are small bands of wandering entertainers, ironworkers, and animal traders who may congregate in communities called *tanda*s. A group variously known as the Banjari or Vanjari (also called Labhani), originally from Rajasthan and related to the Roma (Gypsies) of Europe, roams over large areas of central India and the Deccan, largely as agricultural labourers and construction workers. Many tribal peoples practice similar occupations seasonally. Shepherds, largely of the Gujar caste, practice transhumance in the western Himalayas. In the semiarid and arid regions where agriculture is either impossible or precarious, herders of cattle, sheep, goats, and camels live in a symbiotic relationship with local or nearby cultivators.

• **Hyderabad, India: Labhani women**

Banjari (Labhani) women in festive dress, near Hyderabad, Telangana, India.

© John Isaac

Although less than one-third of India's people live in towns and cities, more than 6,100 places are classified as urban. In general, the proportion is higher in the agriculturally prosperous regions of the northwest, west, and south than in the northeastern rice-growing parts of the country, where the population capacity is limited by generally meagre crop surpluses.

India urban-rural (2018)

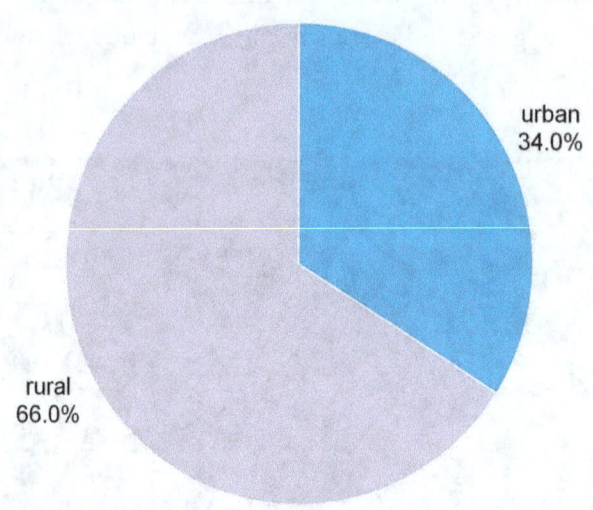

© Encyclopædia Britannica, Inc.

In India large cities long have been growing at faster rates than small cities and towns. The major metropolitan agglomerations have the fastest rates of all, even where, as in Kolkata, there is a high degree of congestion within the central city. Major contributors to urban growth are the burgeoning of the bureaucracy, the increasing commercialization of the agricultural economy, and the spread of factory industry and services.

In many cities dating from the precolonial period, such as Delhi and Agra, the urban core is an exceedingly congested area within an old city wall, portions of which may still stand. In those "old cities," residential segregation by religion and caste and the layout of streets and open places are, except for scale, not greatly dissimilar from what was described above for shapeless agglomerated villages. In contrast to many Western cities, affluent families commonly occupy houses in the heart of the most congested urban wards. Specialized bazaar streets selling sweets, grain, cloth, metalware, jewelry, books and stationery, and other commodities are characteristic of the old city. In such streets it is common for a single building to be at once a workshop, a retail outlet for what the workshop produces, and the residence for the artisan's family and employees.

Moderately old, highly congested urban cores also characterize many cities that grew up in the wake of British occupation. Of those, <u>Kolkata</u>, Mumbai, and <u>Chennai</u> are the most notable examples. In such cases, however, there are usually a few broad major thoroughfares, some degree of regularity to the street pattern, space reserved for parks, and a central business district, including old government offices, high-rise commercial office buildings, banks, elite shopping establishments, restaurants, hotels, museums, a few churches, and other reminders of the former colonial presence.

Associated with a great many cities are special sections created originally for the needs of the British: largely residential areas known as civil lines, where the families of resident European administrators occupied spacious <u>bungalows</u>, with adjoining outbuildings for their servants, nearby shopping facilities, and a <u>gymkhana</u> (a combined sports and social club); cantonments, where military personnel of all ranks were quartered, together with adjacent parade grounds, polo fields, and firing ranges; and industrial zones, including not only the modern mills but also the adjacent "factory lines," reminiscent of 19th-century company housing in <u>Britain</u> but even more squalid.

In the post independence period, with the acceleration of urban growth and the consequent need for <u>urban planning</u>, new forms arose. The millions of refugees from <u>Pakistan</u>, for example, led to the establishment of many "model" (i.e., planned) towns on the edges of the existing cities. The subsequent steady influx of job seekers, together with the natural growth of the already settled population, gave rise to many planned residential areas, typically called "colonies," usually consisting of four- or five-story apartment blocks, a small <u>shopping centre</u>, schools, and playgrounds and other recreational spaces. In general, commuting from colonies to jobs in the inner city is by either bus or bicycle.

For poorer immigrants, residence in those urban colonies was not an option. Some could afford to move into slum flats, often sharing space with earlier immigrants from their native villages. Others, however, had no recourse but to find shelter in *basti*s (<u>shantytowns</u>), clusters of anywhere from a few to many hundreds of makeshift dwellings, which are commonly found along the edges of railroad yards and parks, outside the walls of factories, along the banks of rivers, and wherever else the urban authorities might tolerate their presence. Finally, there are the street dwellers, mainly single men in search of temporary employment, who lack even the meagre shelter that the *basti*s afford.

A special type of urban place to which British rule gave rise were the hill stations, such as <u>Shimla</u> (Simla) and <u>Darjiling</u> (Darjeeling). Those were erected at elevations high enough to provide cool retreats for the dependents of Europeans stationed in India and, in the summer months, to serve as seasonal capitals of the central or provincial governments. Hotels, guest houses, boarding schools, clubs, and other recreational facilities characterize those settlements. Since independence, affluent Indians have come to depend on the hill stations no less than did the British.

India's population is growing rapidly. This has posed many difficulties in the way of economic development. Growing population has forward and backward linkages with the other economic dynamics particularly poverty and unemployment. Raising population is accompanied by a rise in the labor force of the community which leads to the substantial chunk of population to unemployment (Pethe, 1982).

Table 21

- ## Decadal Growth rate of Population, 2001-2011

STATES	RURAL	URBAN	TOTAL
Andhra Pradesh	1.73	35.61	10.98
Arunachal Pradesh	22.56	30.27	26.03
Assam	15.47	27.80	17.07
Bihar	24.25	35.43	25.42
Chhattisgarh	17.78	41.84	22.61
Goa	-18.51	35.23	8.23
Gujrat	9.31	36.00	19.28
Haryana	9.85	44.50	19.90
Himachal Pradesh	12.65	15.61	12.94
Jammu & Kashmir	19.42	36.42	23.64

Jharkhand	19.58	32.36	22.42
Karnataka	7.40	31.54	15.60
Kerala	-25.89	92.76	4.91
Madhya Pradesh	18.42	25.69	20.35
Maharashtra	10.36	23.64	15.99
Manipur	9.14	41.83	18.63
Meghalaya	27.17	31.12	27.95
Mizoram	17,40	29.65	23.48
Nagaland	-14,55	66.57	-0.58
Orissa	11.77	26.94	14.05
Punjab	7.75	25.86	13.89
Rajasthan	18.96	29.01	21.31
Sikkim	-4.99	156.52	12.89
Tamil Nadu	6.61	27.05	15.61
Tripura	2.22	76.17	14.84
Uttarakhand	17.97	28.82	20.23
Uttar Pradesh	11.52	39.94	18.81
West Bengal	7.68	29.72	13.84
UNION TERRITORIES			
Andaman & Nicobar	-1.19	23.40	6.86
Chandigarh	-68.53	26.96	17.19
Dadar & Nagar Haveli	7.70	218.24	55.88

Daman & Diu	-40.12	218.84	53.76
Delhi	-55.64	26.83	21.21
Lakshadweep	-58.02	86.64	6.30
Pondicherry	21.53	31.47	28.08
INDIA	12.25	31.80	17.69

• **Source: Census Of India; 2001 and 2011.**

As a population grows larger, the ability to restore resources for development may grow progressively smaller. This is true for individual nations just as it is true for entire world. Too few people may retard economic development as surely as too many people might. With a limited Gross National Product (GNP) in less developed countries like India, larger the size of population, the smaller will be the per capita income and the lower the level of living standard. It is hard to increase per capita income quickly, it is necessary either to achieve rapid economic growth or to restrict additional population growth (Tiware 2000).

India's population is growing rapidly. This has posed many difficulties in the way of economic development. Growing population has forward and backward linkages with the other economic dynamics particularly poverty and unemployment. Rising population is accompanied by a rise in the labor force of the community which leads the substantial chunk of population to unemployment (Pethe 1982). As a matter of fact, unemployment is that situation, when people are willing to work at the prevailing wage rate, but they don't get work. Hence, it makes the solution of the problem of unemployment more intricate. Obviously, a significant proportion of the national resources will have to be used to expand employment opportunities to absorb the increasing labor force and the backlog of unemployed left over due to the continuous pressure of a rapidly growing population (Dev 2000).

The Table-18 above exhibits the decadal growth of population in India during the period of 2001 and 2011. It is clear from the data in table that during the decade of 2001 and 2011 the population of India grew at the rate of 17.69 per cent. Where the rural population grew at the rate of 12.25 per cent, what we can call moderate growth. As against this, the urban population increased with high tempo of 31.80 per cent during the same period.

Communities that have been historically at the lower end of social groups are also the most disadvantaged in the labor market, found a 2018 <u>study</u> in southern Rajasthan by the Aajeevika Bureau, published in the *Journal of Interdisciplinary Economics*. Over 79% of the migration, mostly by men, in the study was inter-state, with Gujarat as the most popular destination. At the destination, the work was disaggregated based on caste, leaving STs no choice but to work at the lowest end of the labor market. Among ST migrants, more than half worked as helpers and about 30% worked as masons, the study found. Other migrants from the "general" category and OBCs performed more skilled tasks. Migrants from the "general" category have better qualifications for urban job centers, because of the historical advantage of education and are therefore, able to find higher-paying jobs in urban areas. Caste is also a decisive factor among women in deciding the nature of employment and the nature of migration.

Women from SCs and STs often migrate from one rural area to the other because of displacement and loss in the ownership of forest resources, a 2012 <u>study</u> on gender and migration, conducted across 20 states of India by the Centre for Women's Development Studies, Delhi between 2008 and 2011 showed. About 66% of "upper caste" female migrant workers were engaged in white-collar services, as compared to other caste groups– 36% among OBC, 19% among SC, and 18% among ST– the report said. Most tribal women were concentrated in the construction sector, lower-caste women in sectors such as brickmaking and OBC migrant women worked as paid domestic workers and seasonal agricultural workers, according to the report. Of a sample of 1,600 families surveyed in four states, more than three-fourths of migrant tribal women from Chhattisgarh, Jharkhand and Odisha worked as domestic servants while migrant tribal women from Madhya Pradesh were engaged in wage employment, found a 2010 <u>report</u> by the Society for Regional Research and Analysis. The report also found that long- and medium-term female migration was dominated by migrants from the "general" category, while most tribal women migrated for the short or medium term.

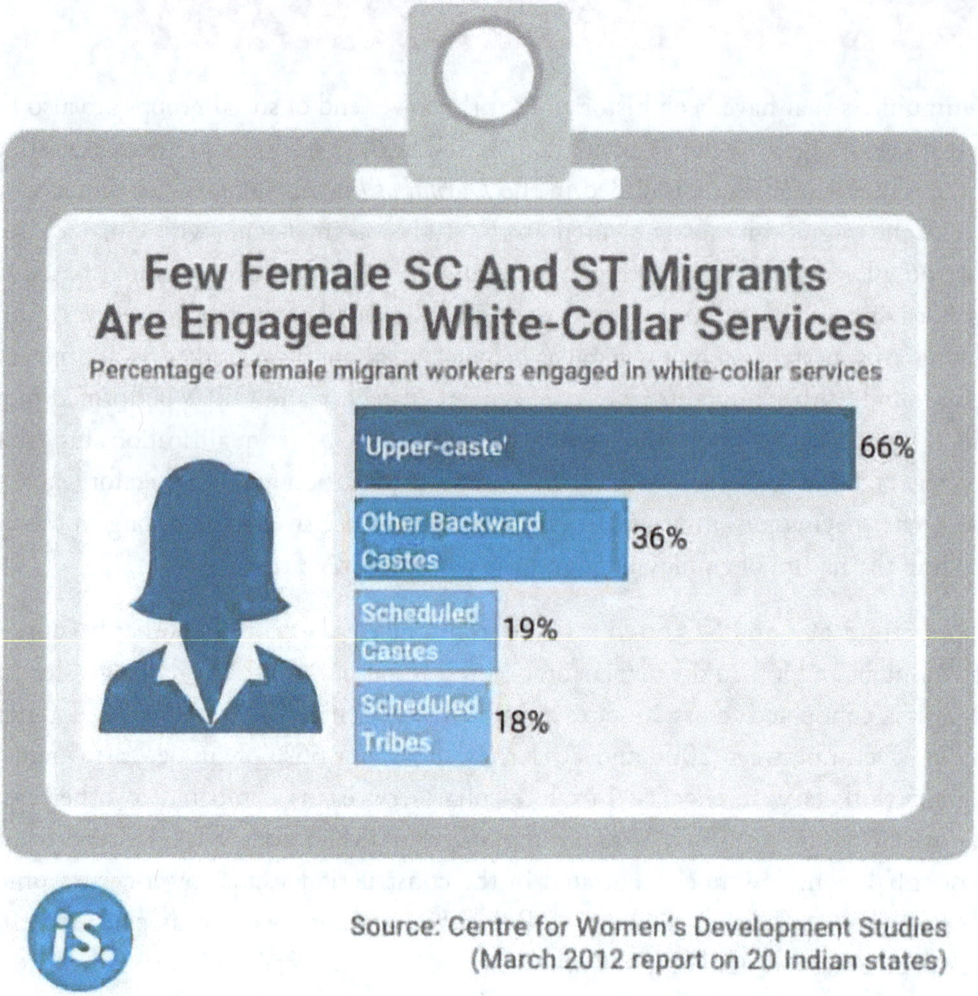

Few Female SC And ST Migrants Are Engaged In White-Collar Services

Percentage of female migrant workers engaged in white-collar services

Category	Percentage
'Upper-caste'	66%
Other Backward Castes	36%
Scheduled Castes	19%
Scheduled Tribes	18%

Source: Centre for Women's Development Studies
(March 2012 report on 20 Indian states)

Emigration patterns In Kerala, even though Hindus are the single largest segment of the state's population, more Muslims emigrate than Hindus. This is because of a history of maritime trade with the Arab region, which began as early as the ninth century and was fueled by the spice trade. In the 1970s, when Kerala had high unemployment, it became lucrative to move to the Gulf region to fill the surge in demand for skilled and unskilled labor. SC/ST community emigration has reduced in Kerala, found eight rounds of the Kerala Migration Survey, conducted by the Centre for Development Studies in Thiruvananthapuram. In 1998, 1.4% of emigrants were from the SC/ST community which reduced to 0.9% in the 2018 survey. Together, SCs and STs make up 3.3% of Kerala's population. The low SC/ST emigration deepens caste inequalities as remittances play a crucial role in Kerala's economy and the prosperity of its population, according to a 2017 study published in *Routledge India*. Even when those from the lower castes emigrate, they face discrimination. As many as a quarter– 26%– of 1,500 Dalits from South Asia interviewed in the United States of America had faced physical violence because of their caste, while 20% reported discrimination at their workplaces, according to a <u>survey</u> conducted in 2016 by Equality Labs, a US-based research organization.

Table 22

· **State-wise Poverty estimates (percent below poverty line) 2004-05 and 2011-12**

STATES/UT'S	YEARS		DECREASE
	2004-05	2011-12	
Andhra Pradesh	29.9	9.2	20.7
Arunachal Pradesh	31.1	34.7	-3.6
Assam	34.4	32.0	2.4
Bihar	54.4	33.7	20.7
Chhattisgarh	49.4	39.9	9.5
Goa	25.0	5.1	19.9
Gujrat	31.8	16.6	15.2
Haryana	24.1	11.2	12.9
Himachal Pradesh	22.9	8.1	14.8
Jammu & Kashmir	13.2	10.4	2.9
Jharkhand	45.3	37.0	8.3
Karnataka	33.4	20.9	12.5
Kerala	19.7	7.1	12.7
Madhya Pradesh	48.6	31.7	17.0

Maharashtra	38.1	17.4	20.8
Manipur	38.0	36.9	1.1
Meghalaya	16.1	11.9	9.2
Mizoram	15.3	20.4	-5.1
Nagaland	9.0	18.9	-9.9
Orissa	57.2	32.6	24.6
Punjab	20.9	8.3	12.6
Rajasthan	34.4	14.7	19.7
Sikkim	31.1	8.2	22.9
Tamil Nadu	28.9	11.3	17.6
Tripura	40.6	14.1	26.6
Uttarakhand	32.7	11.3	21.4
Uttar Pradesh	40.9	29.4	11.5
West Bengal	34.3	20.0	14.3
UNION TERRITORIES			
Delhi	13.1	9.9	3.2
Pondicherry	14.1	9.7	4.4
India	37.2	21.9	15.3

Population below the Poverty Line in India are presented in Table 22 above. The data presented shows the poverty across the different states of India during the period of 2004-05 and 2011-12. The perusal of the data exhibits that during the period of 2004-05 and 2011-12, there was a decline in poverty at all India level

Table 23

· **Poverty Rates**

	SCHEDULED CASTES	SCHEDULED TRIBES	NON-SCHEDULED	ALL
Overall Age	30.1	39.4	17.7	22.7
20–29	26.7	36.6	17.9	22.5
30–39	36.9	45.6	22.7	28.7
40–49	30.5	39.5	17.1	22.4
50–59	23.2	34.0	14.3	18.0
60–70	26.4	33.5	14.0	17.9
HOUSEHOLD SIZE				
1	7.6	11.3	5.0	6.1
2	12.1	18.6	5.1	8.4
3	18.4	26.6	8.6	12.9
4	24.4	33.6	12.9	17.4
5	33.2	42.7	17.5	23.9
6	38.0	49.5	25.1	30.7
7 or more	47.6	56.0	29.0	35.4
EDUCATION				
Not literate	33.4	45.3	24.0	29.5

Literate, below primary	27.8	34.7	17.4	21.2
Literate, below secondary	24.1	27.3	13.4	16.2
Literate, secondary	23.0	14.7	7.9	10.1
Literate, higher secondary and above	13.6	15.9	5.3	6.8
OCCUPATION				
Self-employed in non-agriculture	27.7	34.1	16.3	19.3
Self-employed in agriculture	23.1	32.4	13.2	16.5
Agricultural labor	34.9	48.7	28.6	33.5
Non-agricultural labor	27.1	38.0	17.8	22.5
Others	18.4	19.2	9.9	11.7

Notes: **Observations are weighted by the multipliers assigned to each household in the unit record datafile.**

• *Source*: 55th round (1999/2000) of the consumer expenditure survey of the NSS.

India's Scheduled Castes are distributed across 31 states and union territories. While the 200 million SCs constitute a significant proportion of India's population, the total, if unofficial, number of Scheduled Castes in the country is almost certainly considerably higher, as Christian and Muslim Dalits are not registered as 'Scheduled Castes'. Hence, they are not entitled to so- called reservations in the education system and government jobs and other constitutional safeguards. Dr Umakant, a researcher on Dalit issues, believes that with the rise in population of SCs the Government of India should reorient several of its policies for their overall inclusive development: It should also increase the quantum of reservations in education and jobs and other sectors without any further delay.

The 2011 Census recorded nearly 201.4 million people belonging to various Scheduled Castes in the country. As per the 2001 census, the number was 166.6 million. The Dalit population showed a decadal growth of 20.8 per cent, whereas India's population grew 17.7 per cent during the same period. Although there is an increase in the population of Dalits in the country, many states with a considerable number of Dalits do not have any legislative measures to protect the interests of the community. Dalit empowerment is very poor in many states, many Dalits are landless and efforts to empower them by giving free land have not been successful. Unlike Punjab, which has a considerable number of Dalits as industrialists, other states there is hardly any industrialist from Scheduled Caste community (Sivakumar, 2013). More than three-fourths of India's SCs are still living in rural areas, but since the 2001 census, there has been a 40 per cent increase in the number of SCs living in urban areas. This figure is now approaching 50 million, while more than 150 million still live in rural India (ISDN, 2013). Caste affected Scheduled Caste population in rural settings face a number of serious challenges, including lack of access to resources, land, basic services and justice. Scheduled Caste form a large proportion of India's agricultural workers but they generally do not own land and they are forced to do low-paying and undesirable occupations such as street sweeping and removing human waste and dead animals. They are often not allowed to use the same wells or attend the same temples as higher castes. The landlords' socioeconomic and political power in rural, agricultural areas and status as employers of Dalit allows for continual caste and gender violence. Dalit are met with physical, verbal and sexual violence from the landlords when they try to assert their economic right to wages or land and their right to sexual integrity.

Table 24

· **Scheduled caste and Scheduled Tribes Population 1991 census by States.**

SL. NO	STATES/UT	PERCENT OF SC POPULATION	PERCENT OF ST POPULATION
1	Andhra Pradesh	15.93	6.31
2	Arunachal Pradesh	0.47	63.66
3	Assam	7.40	12.83
4	Bihar	14.56	7.66
5	Chhattisgarh	-	-

6	Goa	2.08	0.03
7	Gujrat	7.41	14.92
8	Haryana	19.75	-
9	Himachal Pradesh	25.34	4.22
10	Jammu & Kashmir	-	-
11	Jharkhand	-	-
12	Karnataka	16.38	4.26
13	Kerala	9.92	1.10
14	Madhya Pradesh	14.54	23.27
15	Maharashtra	11.10	9.27
16	Manipur	2.02	34.41
17	Meghalaya	0.51	85.53
18	Mizoram	0.10	94.75
19	Nagaland	-	87.70
20	Orissa	16.20	22.21
21	Punjab	28.31	-
22	Rajasthan	17.29	12.44
23	Sikkim	5.93	22.36
24	Tamil Nadu	19.18	1.03
25	Tripura	16.36	30.95
26	Uttar Pradesh	21.04	0.21
27	Uttarakhand	-	-

28	West Bengal	23.62	5.60
29	A & N Island	-	9.54
30	Chandigarh	16.51	-
31	D & N Haveli	1.97	78.99
32	Daman & Diu	3.83	11.54
33	NCT of Delhi	19.05	-
34	Puducherry	16.25	-
	INDIA	16.48	8.08

Sex ratio is defined as the number of females per thousand males. It is an important and useful indicator to assess relative excess of deficit of men or women in a given population at that point of time. Among various elements of population composition, sex ratio holds a prime place for population geographers. The separate data for males and females are important for various types of planning and for the analysis of other demographic characteristics, such as mortality, fertility, marital status, economic characteristics, etc. The balance between two sexes affects the social and economic relationship within a community (Chandana, 2006). The various geographical factor influences on the pattern of sex ratio. The ratio of girls to boys (i.e., Sex ratios) in India reveals excess girl child deficit in comparison with developed and many other developing countries.

A forementioned statement shows variation in sex ratio of Scheduled Caste for total, rural and urban areas. Interestingly the sex ratio of Scheduled Castes population shows increasing trends for total, rural and urban population between 2001 and 2011. Despite having lower literacy rates than 'others', Scheduled Caste households have higher sex ratios, and tribals the highest of all. There are around 97.9 million women among the total SC population, As per the 2011 census Scheduled Caste Sex ratio was 936 females for 1,000 males in the same period overall sex ratio was 933/1,000 in 2001 and raised to 945/1,000 of SCs, the overall is to 943/1,000. The sex ratio of Scheduled Caste top states are Kerala (1,057), Pondicherry (1,056), Goa (1,015), Andhra Pradesh (1,008) and Tamil Nadu (1,004) and less performing states are Mizoram (509), Dadra and Nagar Haveli (853), Chandigarh (872), Haryana (887) and NCT Delhi (889). It is observed that the changing attitude about female, increasing employment opportunities for woman, decreasing mortality of females and increasing age of marriage are the major causes of increasing sex ratio among Scheduled Caste. Even though such developments, one can realize the degree of sickness by National Crime Records Bureau report that most of the crimes against SCs reported were crimes against women, including assault harassment, stalking, voyeurism and insult to modesty. 'Majority of cases under crimes against SC women were reported under "Cruelty by Husband or His relatives" (32.6%) followed by "Assault on Women with intent to Outrage her Modesty" (25%), "Kidnapping and Abduction of Women" (19%) and "Rape" (11.5%)' (NCRB, 2017).

Table 25

• **Comparison of Scheduled Caste Sex Ratio and Child Sex Ratio with Overall Population as per 2011 Census**

	SEX RATIO				CHILD SEX RATIO			
	2001		2011		2001		2011	
Indicator	SCs	overall	scs	overall	scs	overall	scs	overall
total	936	933	945	943	938	927	933	919
Rural	939	946	945	949	941	934	936	923
urban	923	900	946	929	924	907	922	905

The child sex ratio is one of the determining factors of population growth. The aforementioned analysis of percentage of child population of Scheduled Castes shows decreasing trend in India. The child sex ratio of Scheduled Caste is 938/1,000 in 2001 and it is fallen to 933/1,000 in 2011 census report in the same year the overall child sex ratio of India was 927/1,000 in 2001 also fallen to 923/1,000 in 2011. State wise child sex ratio of Scheduled Caste: top states are Mizoram (1,161), Goa (982), Jharkhand (976), Sikkim (973) and Pondicherry (969) and less performing states are Jammu and Kashmir (861), Haryana (876), Chandigarh (887), Punjab (888) and NCT Delhi (891). It is observed that the differential in sex composition of rural and urban Scheduled

Caste child population shows wide disparity. It is also observed that sex ratio of rural Scheduled Caste population is higher than urban sex ratio.

Literacy Status of Scheduled Castes

Literacy rate is an important indicator of human development achieved by a society. The progress of any country depends on the nature of education imparted. Article 46 of the Constitution states that, 'The State shall promote, with special care, the education and economic interests of the weaker sections of the people, and, in particular of the Scheduled Castes and Scheduled Tribes, and shall protect them from social injustice and all forms of social exploitation' (Basu, 2012). Even though, Scheduled Castes have lack of access to education. When those education resources are in non-Dalit areas, they are attacked for attempting to use them. When it comes to infrastructure and resources in Dalit communities, the government often overlooks those areas and does not allocate the necessary funds to ensure equality of access to resources. Furthermore, Scheduled Caste women have very limited access to education, which leads to insecurity and lack of access to other resources. In this context the comparative analysis of literacy rate of Scheduled Castes for total, rural and urban areas discussed.

Data shows the literacy rate of Scheduled Caste as per 2011 census. It shows that literacy rate has risen from 54.7 in 2001 to 66.1 in 2011, but the National literacy rate in the same period has risen from 64.8 in 2001 to 73.0 in 2011. State wise Scheduled Caste literacy rate: Daman and Diu (92.6), Mizoram (92.4), Tripura (89.4), Dadra and Nagara Haveli (89.4) and Kerala (88.7) are the top five states in SCs Literacy rate and Bihar (48.5), Jharkhand (55.9), Rajasthan (59.7), Uttar Pradesh (60.9) and Andhra Pradesh (62.3) are the bottom five states in Scheduled Caste literacy rate during the 2011 census. There has been a significant increase in overall literacy rates across the country since the early 1990s. Gender and social disparities have also declined with an overall increase in school attendance. Even though there is growth in literacy level, still Scheduled Caste people have the highest poverty levels, are land less and depend on the dominant caste for employment, wages and loans. A report by The India Governs Research Institute says nearly half of the school dropouts in the primary section happen to be Dalits. Figures show that as many as 138,000 Dalit children dropped out of school within 2 years of their enrolment as against a total of 290,000 dropouts in Karnataka state. In other words, 48 per cent of dropouts are from Dalit communities. As sociologist Prof G. K. Karanth said 'Backwardness of the north Karnataka region, poverty and migration for employment contribute to the higher dropout rate among Dalits' (Times of India, 2014). It is found that major reason for drop out for males is 'engaged in economic activities'; for females the reason is 'engaged in domestic activities' for rural as well as urban SCs (MOSPI, 2014).

Migration patterns and its impacts are based on a household's caste, found a 2016 study from Beed in Maharashtra, published in the *Social Science Spectrum*. For Dalits, Ban- jari's and Muslim migrants, sugarcane cutting was a long-term, permanent activity undertaken for generations. For dominant castes, such as the Marathas, it was undertaken for a couple of years in response to shocks or crises. In India, a 'dominant caste' refers to "a single caste in a specified region that usually has control or ownership of most of the agricultural land, is numerically significant, and as a result, holds a dominant position in that region".Whether migration leads to accumulation of wealth or not is also influenced by caste, networks, and land possessed, Kalyani Var- tak, the author of the Beed study, concluded, based on her assessment of intergenerational migration in different caste communities. Families that were only seasonally involved in sugarcane cutting were better off than those involved in the job permanently, the study found.

There are overlaps between a migrant's social and economic status. People from the general category and Other Backward Classes (OBC) have higher chances of migrating and bearing the cost of migration. The disadvantaged castes are often unable to gain the benefits of migration. Migration pays off if the worker is from a higher caste, found a 2018 study linking caste and job market participation among migrants in the slum areas of four Indian cities—Ludhiana, Ujjain, Mathura and Jaipur.

CHAPTER VI.

SOCIAL SEGREGATION OF THE LABOR MARKET

Communities that have been historically at the lower end of social groups are also the most disadvantaged in the labor market, found a 2018 study in southern Rajasthan by the Aajeevika Bureau, published in the *Journal of Interdisciplinary Economics*. Over 79% of the migration (mostly men) in the study was inter-state, with Gujarat as the most popular destination. At the destination, the work was disaggregated based on caste, leaving STs no choice but to work at the lowest end of the labor market. Among ST migrants, more than half worked as helpers and about 30% worked as masons, the study found. Other migrants from the 'general' category and OBCs performed more skilled tasks.

Migrants from the 'general' category have better qualifications for urban job centers, because of the historical advantage of education and are therefore able to find higher-paying jobs in urban areas. Caste is also a decisive factor among women in deciding the nature of employment and the nature of migration. Women from SCs and STs often migrate from one rural area to the other because of displacement and loss in the ownership of forest resources, a 2012 study on gender and migration, conducted across 20 states of India by the Centre for Women's Development Studies, Delhi between 2008 and 2011 showed. About 66% of 'upper caste' female migrant workers were engaged in white-collar services, as compared to other caste groups–OBC (36%), SC (19%), and ST (18%)–the report said.

Table 26

· Percentage of Scheduled Caste (SC's) and Scheduled Tribes (ST) Population in 2001 & 2011

SL NO	STATES/UT	SC		ST	
		2001	2011	2001	2011
1	Andhra Pradesh	18.4	19.2	8.4	9.3
2	Arunachal Pradesh	0.4	-	69.7	74.1
3	Assam	6.7	6.8	13.6	13.7
4	Bihar	16.4	16.6	1.0	1.4
5	Chhattisgarh	11.4	12.8	37.6	36.9
6	Goa	1.6	1.7	0.0	15.9
7	Gujrat	6.9	6.6	21.6	23.1
8	Haryana	21.4	22.5	-	-
9	Himachal Pradesh	25.6	26.0	4.3	6.1
10	Jammu & Kashmir	8.3	8.2	13.8	15.4
11	Jharkhand	12.4	12.6	31.0	31.4
12	Karnataka	18.4	20.0	8.4	9.2
13	Kerala	10.8	10.4	1.5	2.5
14	Madhya Pradesh	15.6	15.7	25.8	27.2
15	Maharashtra	10.9	12.2	13.4	14.6
16	Manipur	1.3	2.7	44.4	45.6
17	Meghalaya	0.4	0.5	90.2	90.1

18	Mizoram	0.0	0.1	96.3	96.6
19	Nagaland	-	-	93.7	92.8
20	Orissa	17.2	17.8	24.6	25.7
21	Punjab	33.0	37.5	-	-
22	Rajasthan	17.9	18.5	15.5	16.9
23	Sikkim	5,0	4.4	21.2	36.6
24	Tamil Nadu	23.8	25.5	1.6	1.8
25	Tripura	17.2	16.1	36.5	41.2
26	Uttar Pradesh	23.4	23.0	0.1	0.7
27	Uttarakhand	19.9	21.3	3.8	3.8
28	West Bengal	26.9	27.5	7.2	7.8
29	A & N Island	-	-	11.9	11.3
30	Chandigarh	16.0	17.2	-	-
31	D & N Haveli	1.7	0.7	74.9	82.4
32	Daman & Diu	2.9	3.6	11.1	12.6
33	NCT of Delhi	19.9	19.6	-	-
34	Puducherry	27.2	27.9	-	-
	INDIA	17.9	18.5	10.4	11.3

- Source: Census of India.

Rural poverty is largely a result of low productivity and unemployment. The Jawahar Rozgar Yojana, a national public works scheme launched in 1989 with financing from the central and state governments, provides more than, 700-million-person days of work a year about 1% of total employment for people with few opportunities for employment. The scheme has two components: a program to provide low-cost housing and one to supply free irrigation wells to poor and marginalized farmers. The public works scheme is self-targeting. Since it offers employment at the statutory minimum wage for unskilled manual labor, only those willing to accept very low wages the poor are likely to enroll in the scheme. By providing regular employment and thereby increasing the bargaining power of all rural workers, the public works scheme has had a significant effect in reducing poverty. It has also contributed to the construction of rural infrastructure (irrigation works, a soil conservation project, drinking water supply). Evaluations show that 82% of available funds have been channeled to community development projects. Targeting was improved in 1996 when the housing and irrigation well components were delinked and focused exclusively on people below the poverty line.

Most tribal women were concentrated in the construction sector, lower-caste women in sectors such as brickmaking, and OBC migrant women worked as paid domestic workers and seasonal agricultural workers, according to the report. Of a sample of 1,600 families surveyed in four states, more than three-fourths of migrant tribal women from Chhattisgarh, Jharkhand and Odisha worked as domestic servants while migrant tribal women from Madhya Pradesh were engaged in wage employment, found a 2010 report by the Society for Regional Research and Analysis. The report also found that long-and medium-term female migration was dominated by migrants from the 'general' category, while most tribal women migrated for the short or medium term.

Table 27

- ## Poverty Ratio by States in India 2011-2020

States	YEAR (% BELOW POVERTY LINE)			
	2020	2004-05	2011-12	Decrease
Andhra Pradesh	3.9	29.9	9.2	20.7
Arunachal Pradesh	-	31.1	34.7	-3.6
Assam	1.6	34.4	32.0	2.4
Bihar	11.5	54.4	33.7	20.7
Chhattisgarh	6.2	49.4	39.9	9.5
Delhi	8.0	13.1	9.9	3.2
Goa	21.1	25.0	5.1	19.9
Gujrat	3.2	31.8	16.6	15.2
Haryana	26.4	24.1	11.2	12.9
Himachal Pradesh	15.1	22.9	8.1	14.8
Jammu & Kashmir	14.2	13.2	10.4	2.9
Jharkhand	12.1	45.3	37.0	8.3
Karnataka	2.5	33.4	20.9	12.5
Kerala	4.3	19.7	7.1	12.7
Madhya Pradesh	2.1	48.6	31.7	17.0
Maharashtra	3.8	38.1	17.4	20.8
Manipur	-	38.0	36.9	1.1
Meghalaya	3.8	16.1	11.9	9.2

Mizoram	-	15.3	20.4	-5.1
Nagaland	-	9.0	18.9	-9.9
Orissa	2.5	57.2	32.6	24.6
Punjab	7.2	20.9	8.3	12.6
Rajasthan	25.6	34.4	14.7	19.7
Sikkim	4.3	31.1	8.2	22.9
Tamil Nadu	4.8	28.9	11.3	17.6
Tripura	11.1	40.6	4.1	26.6
Uttarakhand	4.7	32.7	11.3	21.4
Uttar Pradesh	4.1	40.9	29.4	11.5
West Bengal	6.2	34.3	20.0	14.3
UNION TERRITORIES				
Andaman & Nicobar	-	-	-	-
Chandigarh	-	-	-	-
Dadar & Nagar Haveli	-	-	-	-
Daman & Diu	-	-	-	-
Delhi	-	13.1	9.9	3.2
Lakshadweep	-	-	-	-
Pondicherry	-	14.1	9.7	4.4
INDIA	8.8	37.2	21.9	15.3

• Source: Review of Expert Group to Review the Methodology for Estimation of Poverty (2009). Planning Commission, Government of India, 2011-12, 2013

These estimates clearly show that in the first three decades of planning (1951-81) economic growth did not have any impact on the poverty problem in India. This is because of not only slow rate of economic growth during this period but also that benefits of whatever economic growth occurred did not trickle down to the poor. It is only in the eighties and nineties when annual rate of economic growth rate accelerated to around 5.6 per cent and 6 per cent respectively and special employment schemes were started on a large scale that there was a significant decline in the incidence of poverty.

Table 28

· **Trends in Poverty in India**

PERIOD	PERCENTAGE OF POPULATION BELOW THE POVERTY LINE (HCR)			NUMBER OF POOR (IN MILLION)		
	RURAL	URBAN	TOTAL	RURAL	URBAN	TOTAL
1951-55	54.77	42.70	52.66	170.6	28.1	198.7
1965-66	53.96	47.06	52.74	184.6	34.8	219.5
1961-65	48.59	45.46	48.02	183.0	38.6	221.6
1966-70	60.44	50.90	58.60	251.0	50.7	301.7
1973-74	56.4	49.0	54.9	261	60	321
1977-78	53.1	45.2	51.3	264	68	329
1983	45.7	40.8	44.5	252	71	323
1987-88	39.1	38.2	38.9	232	75	307
1993-94	37.3	32.4	36.3	244	76	320

In the eighties of the 20th century, two Five Year Plans, the Sixth Plan (1989-85) and Seventh Plan (1985-90) were launched. In the Sixth Plan period (1980-85) and Seventh Plan period (1985- 90), average annual growth rates of 5.4 per cent and 5.8 per cent respectively were recorded. This higher growth rate in national income also resulted in a higher growth rate in per capita income of 3.2 per cent and 3.6 in the Sixth Plan and Seventh Plan period respectively.

A favorable result of this higher growth rate in both national income and per capita income was the decline in the ratio of people living below the poverty line. As will be seen from Table 25 percentage of population living below the poverty line (All India) which was 51.3 in 1977-78 fell to 44.5 in 1983 and further to 38.9 in 1987-88 and 36.3 in 1993-94. Now, the question is what caused this acceleration in growth rate in the late seventies and the eighties. The important factor causing this acceleration in growth rate in the late seventies and early eighties was the increase in public sector investment which remained sluggish from earlier since the mid-sixties.

Among other factors bringing about higher growth rate is the liberalization measures of removal of some restrictions and relaxation of licensing procedures by making amendments through industrial policy statements of July 1980 and December 1985. In these industrial policy statements certain changes were made in the industrial licensing policies and procedures which were designed to facilitate capacity expansion in the private sector and create a competitive environment. In the latter half of eighties (1985-90), contrary to the Mahalanobis strategy of growth, export promotion was given relatively more importance than import substitution which led to higher growth rates of exports of9.4 percent, 24.1 percent, 15.6 per cent, and 18.9 per cent in 198687, 1987-88, 1988-89 and 1989-90 respectively which speeded up the overall growth rate of the Indian economy during the latter half of the eighties.

But the higher growth rate achieved in the eighties was not sustainable as public sector investment was increased by incurring higher doses of deficit financing leading to higher rates of inflation in the economy and through commercial borrowing on a large scale from abroad which significantly raised external public debt. External public debt servicing consumed a large part of our export earnings. This created foreign exchange crisis in 1990-91 which brought India to the brink of default.

Since capital-intensive technologies were used in the growth process of both industrial and agricultural sectors, the employment opportunities increased but were not large enough to absorb even annual growth of labor force in productive employment. As a result, the backlog of unemployment went on increasing with each successive Five-Year Plan. At the end of Fourth Plan period (1973-74) unemployment was estimated at 9 per cent of labor force on current daily basis.

Rates of gross saving and capital formation as a per cent of GDP, which are important determinants of economic growth showed upward trends with some fluctuations during the period 1951-80. Both rates increased from around 8 per cent in 1950-51 to 13 per cent in 1955-56, the beginning of the second Five Year Plan. Thus the two rates remained in balance during this period (see Table 41.4). However, from 1956 to 1965-66, the gap between the two emerged; gross domestic saving (GDS) falling short of gross domestic capital formulation (GDCF). Besides, the two rates fluctuated a good deal during the decade of 1956-1965. The deficit of gross domestic saving and gross domestic capital formation (GDCF), i.e., gross domestic investment during this decade, was met mostly by obtaining concessional foreign assistance with net capital inflow as percentage of GDFC being equal to 2.12 during 1956-60 and 2.26 during 1961-65. As will be seen from Table 26, during the periods 1966-70 and 1971-73, annual rate of gross domestic capital formation (GDCF) increased to 15 per cent of GDP in 1966-70 and to 15.50 per cent of GDP in 1971-73. This was largely financed by domestic saving which increased only a little.

The average annual rate of gross domestic saving rose from about 13.2 per cent during 1966-70 to 14.7 per cent during 1971-73. It is mainly due to stagnation of gross capital formation during 1966-70 and 1971-73 that average annual rate of growth of GDP during this period fell to 2.9 per cent per annum during 1966-70 and 1.9 per cent during 1971-73 (See Table 26). It may be further noted that after war with Pakistan in 1965 on Kashmir issue and then in 1971 on Bangladesh issue, India could not get much foreign aid. As a result, capital inflow during this period declined, which also accounted for the low rate of capital formation.

Table 29

· Rate of GDS, GDCF and Rate of Growth GDP, from 1951 to 1991

PERIOD	GDS AS% OF GDP AT CURRENT MARKET PRICE	GDCF AS% OF GDP	NET CAPITAL INFLOW (+) AS % GDP	RATE OF GROWTH OF GDP AT 1993-94 PRICE
1951-55	8.74	8.96	0.22	3.85
1956-60	11.10	13.22	2.12	3.38
1961-65	11.96	14.22	2.26	5.00
1966-70	13.18	15.00	1.82	2.90
1970-73	14.67	15.50	0.83	1.90
1974-80	18.60	18.46	-0.14	3.40
1981-85	18.36	19.70	1.34	5.66
1986-90	20.26	22.60	2.34	5.84
1990-91	23.10	26.30	3.20	5.30

From the mid-seventies public sector investment was raised which resulted in higher average rate of capital formation (18.5 per cent of GDP) during 1974-80 and this was fully financed by domestic saving which shot up to 18.6 per cent per annum during this period. In the first half of the eighties, the average annual rate of GDCF as per cent of GDP picked up to 19.7 and in the second half (1986-90) of the eighties to 22.6.

As a result, the annual average growth rate of GDP rose to 5.6 per cent during 1986-90) and to 5.8 per cent during 1986-90. However, in the second half of the eighties (1986-90) annual rate of gross domestic saving (GDS) as per cent of GDPFC was 20.26 resulting in capital inflow of 2.34 per cent of GDPFC which was mostly in the form of commercial borrowing from abroad. This led to a sharp increase in external foreign debt which put pressure on our balance of payments. In 1990-91, the gap between GDS and GDCF widened and resulted in capital inflow of 3.2 per cent of GDPFC causing foreign exchange crisis.

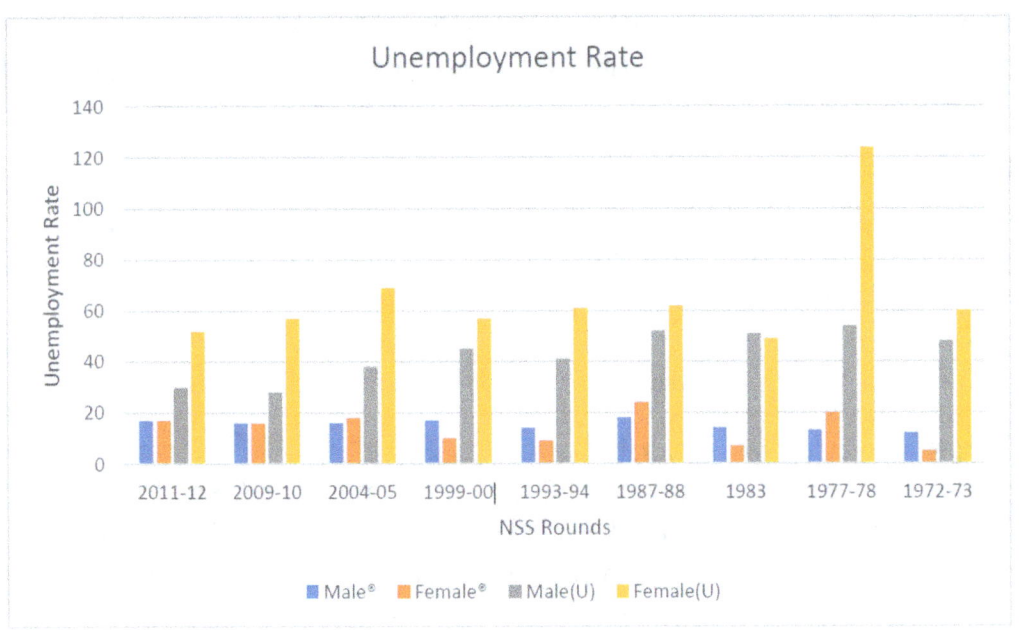

· Emigration impacted by Caste

In Kerala, even though Hindus are the single largest segment of the state's population, more Muslims emigrate than Hindus. This is because of a history of maritime trade with the Arab region which began as early as the ninth century and was fueled by the spice trade. In the 1970s, when Kerala had high unemployment, it became lucrative to move to the Gulf region to fill the surge in demand for skilled and unskilled labor. SC/ST community emigration has reduced in Kerala, found eight rounds of the Kerala Migration Survey, conducted by the Centre for Development Studies in Trivandrum. In 1998, 1.4% of emigrants were from the SC/ST community which reduced to 0.9% in the 2018 survey. Together, SCs and STs make up 3.3% of Kerala's population. The low SC/ST emigration deepens caste inequalities as remittances play a crucial role in Kerala's economy and the prosperity of its population, according to a 2017 study published in *Routledge India.*

Even when those from the lower castes emigrate, they face discrimination. As many as a quarter (26%) of 1,500 Dalits from South Asia interviewed in the United States of America had faced physical violence because of their caste, while 20% reported discrimination at their work-

places, according to a survey conducted in 2016 by Equality Labs, a US-based research organization. The survey also found that 40% of the respondents were made to feel unwelcome at their place of worship, 40% said they were rejected as romantic partners because of their caste and 60% had experienced caste-based derogatory jokes and comments.

It is tougher for female emigrants, who often face violence and abuse at destination countries and are unable to reach out for help as many are isolated as domestic workers in households, said Sister Lissy, the founder of the National Workers Movement, a Hyderabad-based non-governmental organization that works for the welfare of female emigrants. "However, over the years, awareness among women migrants has increased and made them more confident."

The government released the Draft Emigration Bill 2019, which aims at promoting and protecting the welfare of emigrants. This Bill aims to change the Acts of 1922 and 1983 where the focus was to control and regulate all the stakeholders involved in the process of emigration. But the new draft remains detached from social realities as it does not consider the rights of migrants. This leaves migrants at the lowest rungs of the social hierarchy unprotected.

Although we do not have employment trends from National Sample Survey Office (NSSO) after 2011-12, anecdotal evidence suggests that India's job challenge might have worsened in this period. The slow pace of job creation inflicts greater suffering on the workforce in an economy. This suffering, however, is not the same for all workers. Scheduled Castes (SCs), who are at the bottom of the social ladder in India, are among the worst sufferers. Entrenched social discrimination and existing socio-economic realities add to the disadvantages faced by SCs in the labor market. SCs have the lowest land— the most important productive asset— ownership in India. This makes them more dependent on wage labor. Statistics prove this point.

Table 30

- **Population and Decadal Growth Rates of SC, ST and Total Rural Population (1981,1991,2001 and 2011), All India**

CENSUS	POPULATION (NUMBER IN LAKHS)			DECADAL GROWTH RATES (%)		
	Total*	SC	ST	Total*	SC	ST
1981	5238.66	912.05	504.48	-	-	-

1991	6286.91	1123.43	627.51	20.01	23.18	24.39
2001	7410.00	1330.11	773.39	17.86	18.40	23.25
2011	8330.80	1538.50	938.19	17.64	15.70	21.30

• **Source: Planning Commission, Tenth Five Year plan, 2002-07, Volume-II and NSSO, Unit Level data on Employment and Unemployment.**

According to the 2011-12 NSSO statistics, the share of wage laborers among SCs was 63%. This is significantly higher than the values for other social groups. These figures were 44% for Other Backward Classes (OBCs), 42% for upper castes and 46% for the rest. Even among wage laborers, SCs have a much greater share of casual wage workers, which signifies higher job insecurity and poor earnings. The share of casual wage labor was 47 percent for SCs compared with one third for OBC/higher caste/rest, and all India average. In fact, of the total casual laborers in the country, about 32 percent are SC, which is double their population share of 16 percent.

The disadvantage faced by SCs extends beyond their disproportionate dependence on wage work. Because SCs face caste-based discrimination in hiring, they also have a greater unemployment rate than the rest of the population. According to the latest NSSO statistics, the unemployment rate among SCs was 1.7 percentage points higher than the all-India average. SCs have had the highest unemployment rate in India since the 1990s. Higher unemployment among SCs can be seen for young workers and workers with similar levels of education. This underlines the fact that it is a systemic problem.

Why is the unemployment rate higher among SCs when compared with OBCs and higher castes? Economic research points towards the discrimination of SC workers in hiring in the private sector. Dr Bhima Rao Ambedkar argued in Annihilation of caste (1936) that the restriction on SCs to take the occupation of high castes will reduce their chances of employment. The SCs who are denied access to occupation of higher castes suffer from the (non-voluntary) unemployment due to restriction in hiring. The high caste on the other hand would avoid working in an occupation other than that their own and would face unemployment voluntarily. However, the magnitude of non -voluntary unemployment for SCs is likely to be much greater than voluntary unemployment of higher castes. The data on employment brings out this feature of Indian labor market.

Table 31

- Literacy Rates of Scheduled Caste and Scheduled Tribes – Sex Wise- All India-Rural

YEAR	SCHEDULED CASTE			SCHEDULED TRIBES		
	MALE	FEMALE	TOTAL	MALE	FEMALE	TOTAL
1961	15.06	2.52	8.89	13.37	2.90	8.16
1971	20.04	5.06	12.77	16.92	4.36	10.68
1981	27.91	8.45	18.48	22.94	6.81	14.92
1991	45.95	19.45	33.25	38.45	16.02	27.38
2001	63.66	37.84	51.16	57.39	32.44	45.02
2009-10	73.0	52.1	62.8	70.7	52.1	61.6
2011	72.6	52.6	62.8	66.8	46.9	56.9

- Source: GOI, NSSO, Primary Data, 2009-10.

About 72 percent of rural SC population resides in the seven states of Andhra Pradesh, Bihar, Madhya Pradesh, Maharashtra, Rajasthan, Uttar Pradesh and West Bengal. As far as ST's are concerned

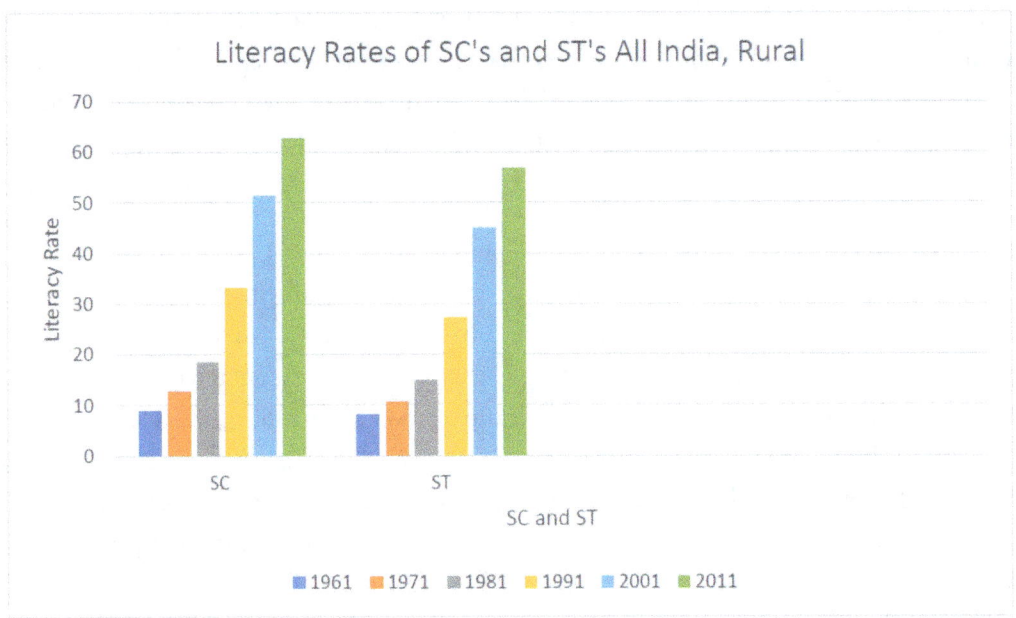

Literacy Rates of SC's and ST's All India, Rural

The 2011-12 NSSO survey shows that SCs are employed for lesser number of days compared with upper castes. A joint paper published this year in the Journal for Social Inclusion Studies has decomposed the difference in employment rate between SCs and upper castes, attributable to differences in human capital endowment (such as education and skill) and those attributable to discrimination in the labor market for the year 2011-12. While endowment differences accounted for around one-third of the employment rate, two-thirds of it were due to discrimination against SCs in the hiring process.

A primary survey conducted by the Indian Institute of Dalit Studies gives us some insights into the nature of caste-based discrimination in employment. The survey was carried out among 1992 households in 80 villages across the states of Maharashtra, Tamil Nadu, Haryana and Uttar Pradesh in 2013. A study of 441 farm wage laborers indicates that about 41 per cent were denied work by the high castes due to caste prejudice. Of these, about 76 percent in grain harvesting, 20 percent in vegetable cultivation and 12 percent in drying of grains and chilly and 11 percent in domestic work were denied jobs, due to 'polluting statuses of the untouchables.

About 71 percent of SC farm wage worker reported a loss of an average of 43 workdays due to discrimination in hiring. Similar discrimination is faced by the SC non-farm wage laborers. Of the total 389 non-farm wage workers, about 52 per cent reported denial of work due to caste background. The caste restrictions are mostly in domestic work such as cooking at high caste homes, serving food in restaurants, work in construction of temples and cultural and religious ceremonies. The average annual loss of employment in number of days in the survey year was about 28.

The regular SC salaried workers in the rural private sector also face discrimination in hiring. Of the 314 regular salaried workers, about 18 percent SCs reported discrimination in selection. About 22 percent reported high caste employers giving preference to persons of their own caste in employment and about 23 percent said high caste persons being selected with less qualification. The studies on the urban labor market also observed discrimination in hiring.

A study by Thorat and Attewell in 2010 observed that for equally qualified SC and upper caste (about 4800 each) applicants, SCs had 67 percent less chance of receiving calls for an interview. What is more disturbing is that the high percentage of less qualified high castes (undergraduate) received calls compared with the more qualified SCs (post-graduates). There are other studies by economists such as Ashwani Deshpande that observed discrimination being faced by SCs in hiring in urban areas. The discrimination against SCs in hiring results in high unemployment, low income and high poverty. For instance, in 2011-12, about one third of the SCs were poor compared with 20 percent OBCs and 9 percent upper castes.

The discrimination in employment not only results in high poverty among SCs, but it also hampers economic growth in the private economy. Standard economic theory tells us that for optimum growth, the perfect mobility of labor and capital is necessary. Discrimination based on castes, leads to an imperfect and segmented labor market. This reduces overall productivity. This calls for affirmative action policies for securing non-discriminatory access to SCs in hiring. Affirmative action for SC labor would assume the form of reservation in jobs or similar policies. An affirmative action policy is also necessary to remove restrictions on labor and capital mobility to promote competition and optimum economic growth.

· **Equality movements can minimize the impact of caste in migration:**

Movements, such as the Ravidassia movement in Punjab (which combined the tenets of Sant Ravidass's teachings with Ambedkar's beliefs), help those belonging to disadvantaged communities access education, hospitals/clinics and safe social spaces. The movement has also helped these communities gain more from migration, a 2008 study published in the *Journal of Asian Studies* showed. Ravidass *deras* (small organizations dedicated to a cause) were pivotal in disseminating the messages of an assertive identity across villages through songs, literature, and poetry especially among the Chamar community, caste believed to be 'lower' caste, which had been one of the most marginalized in Punjab.

The movement, however, could not manage to gain a stronghold in the Malwa and Majha regions of Punjab.

The Doaba region of Punjab has the highest percentage of Dalits and is the source for the highest proportion of overseas migrants from Punjab, 2011 census data show. Punjabi migration in Spain began in the mid-1980s because of friendlier migrant policies in southern Europe in comparison with central European nations such as Germany, which remained conservative in terms of their labor market. The three main caste groups that migrate to Spain are Lubanas (a mer- chant/trader community), Jats (a dominant landowning group), and Ravidassia Chamars (lower caste community), a 2010 study conducted in Catalonia, published in *Routledge*, shows. The Rav- idassia movement led to better socio-economic indicators for the Chamar community in the Doaba region where the movement originated. However, the Chamar community continues to be disadvantaged as compared to other castes because of low land ownership.

Therefore, a number of employment generation unlike the class of landless laborers, the proportion of laborer households with some cultivated land was not very different: 8% in 1970-71 and 10.5% in 1956-57. Here the difference is largely due to the arbitrary figure—the smallest of 10% of the weaker section, while the second A.L.E. had an income criterion for selection. Consequently, one finds the agricultural laborers in Punjab, Haryana and Rajasthan in 1956-57 forming a much smaller proportion of rural households than in 1970-71 while those in States like Bihar, Orissa, Andhra Pradesh and Tamil Nadu much more. Besides this arbitrariness, it is possible, on the grounds stated in para 9 above, to presume that the class of agricultural laborer's, in 1970-71 defined as in the 2nd A.L.E. would, form a larger percentage of the cultivating households in 197071 than in 1956-57. All in all, it is not improper to conclude from this that the coverages of the two surveys, the 2nd A.L.E. and the 25th round 'weaker section', are largely comparable.

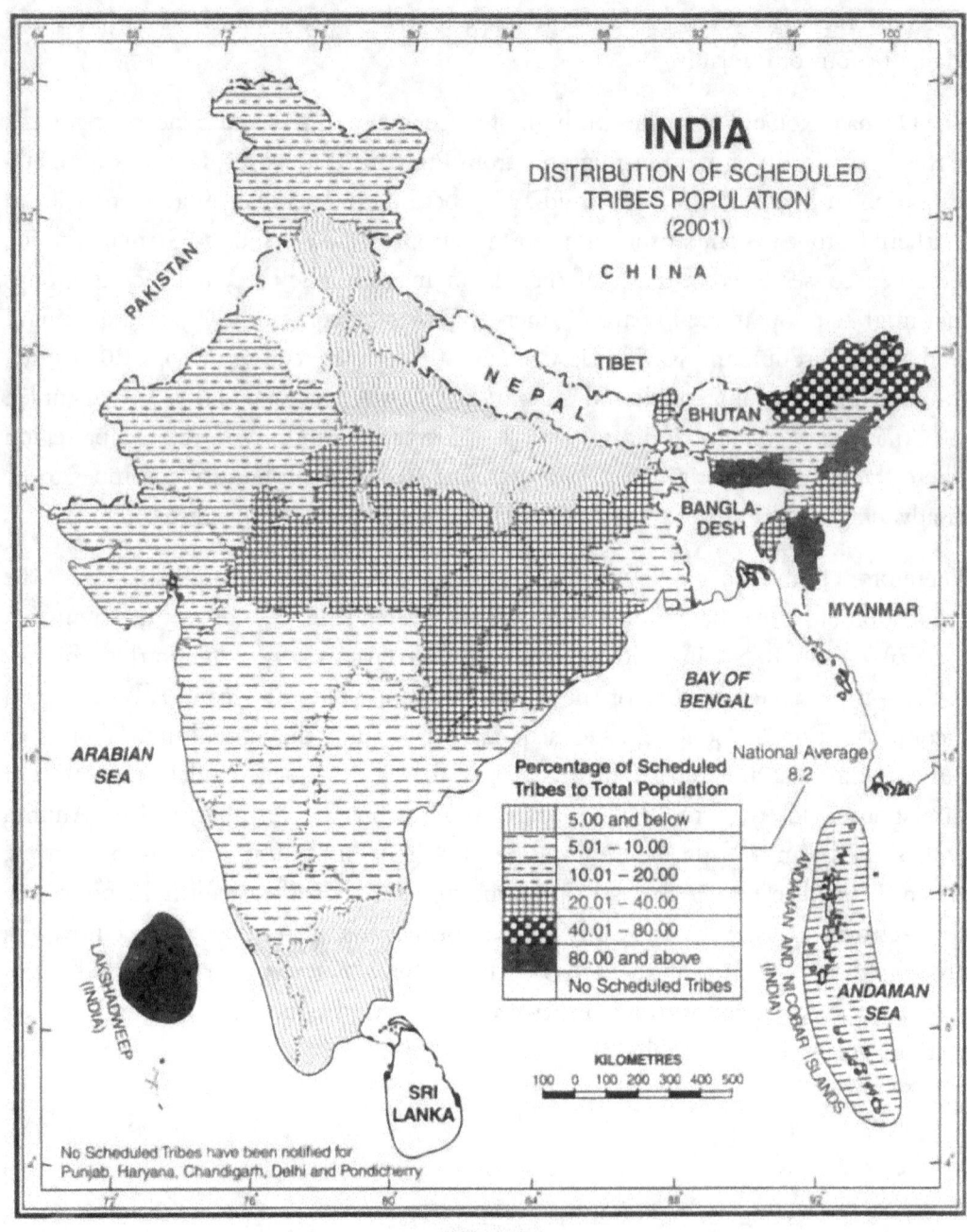

INDIA
DISTRIBUTION OF SCHEDULED
TRIBES POPULATION
(2001)

National Average
8.2

Percentage of Scheduled
Tribes to Total Population

	5.00 and below
	5.01 – 10.00
	10.01 – 20.00
	20.01 – 40.00
	40.01 – 80.00
	80.00 and above
	No Scheduled Tribes

KILOMETRES
100 0 100 200 300 400 500

No Scheduled Tribes have been notified for
Punjab, Haryana, Chandigarh, Delhi and Pondicherry

FIG. 11.3

The 25th round of N.S.S. gives data on total time spent by persons in the small cultivators and landless labor households in gainful employment, in seeking job and in not being available for gainful employment, classified by age and sex. We shall confine ourselves to the adult males between ages 15 and 59 only. The children, that is those under 15 years, are by and large outside the labor market. The same cannot be said about all people aged 60 or above; but for meaningful assessment and comparison, we shall exclude them also. Female employment and particularly unemployment, are more difficult to assess and so we shall keep it aside for our purpose. Table 15 summarizes the total time disposition of the adult males in the 'weaker section' households. It shows that the adult males spent 82% of their normal working hours during the year 1970-71 in gainful employment (on own business or wage labor). Only 5.7% of their total time was spent in unemployment, i.e., in seeking work or being available for work. The remaining 12.5% of the time they were not available for work due to sickness, domestic work, festivities, etc. Only in 5 of the 14 States for which data are available, was the percentage of time spent in unemployment larger than 5.7; Andhra Pradesh, Bihar, Kerala, Punjab and Tamil Nadu. The average percentage of time spent in unemployment was even smaller—3.4%–among the small cultivators, and only a little larger—6.5%–among the landless laborers. For most of the States the averages were less than these all-India averages. Indeed, for some States like Orissa, Madhya Pradesh and Mysore, and Assam and U.P. as well, the time spent by the adult male workers in unemployment was quite small; less than 1 or 2 per cent.

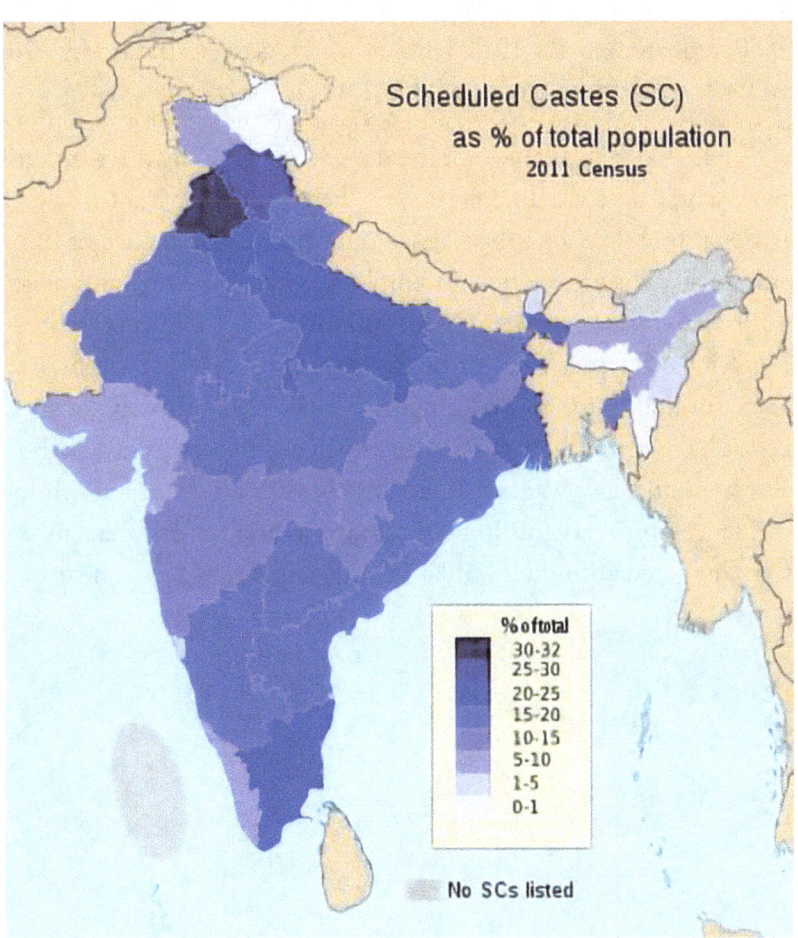

The above findings of the 25th round of the N.S.S. run counter to the general impressions or presumptions about the extent of available employment and prevailing unemployment in the rural areas of the country in general and in some of the States in particular which are among the poorest in India. Indeed, while 4 or 5% unemployment may be quite high by standard of the developed countries, it may not acquire the same significance in rural India if it is remembered that this measures not chronically unemployed persons, but total time spent in unemployment by all the adult males in the 'weaker section' population.

UNEMPLOYMENTSITUATION: In 2000, the CDS employment rate in rural areas was 46% for SC male workers, compared with 48.40% for other male workers. Similarly, the CDS employment rate for SC workers in urban area was 45.8%, compared to49.9% for other households. Disparities between the SC and others are also reflected in the unemployment rate. The unemployment rate based on CDS for SCs was about5.0% as compared to about 3.5% for other workers in rural and urban areas. The NSSO data on wage earning revealed disparities in labor wages for SCs and others. For instance, in 1999–2000, the average weekly wage earning of an SC worker (in 1993– 94 price) was Rs 174.50compared to Rs 197.05 for other workers (estimate by Dubey 2003, Department for International Development [DFID] study).

ECONOMIC STATUS: Available empirical evidence suggests discrimination against SCs in employment, wages, credit, and so on. These factors have acted as constraints to their occupational mobility. In urban areas, too, there is prevalence of discrimination by caste; particularly discrimination in employment, which operates at least in part through traditional mechanisms; SCs are disproportionately represented in poorly paid, dead-end jobs. Further, there is a flawed, preconceived notion that they lack merit and are unsuitable for formal employment.6.32.Due to the lack of access to fixed sources of income and high incidence of wage labor associated with high rate of under-employment and low wages, SC households are often faced with low incomes and high incidence ofpoverty.In2004–05, about 36.80% of SC persons were BPL in rural areas as compared to only 28.30% for others (non-SC/ST). In urban areas the gap was slightly larger.

Table 32

• Literacy Rates* of Scheduled Caste and Scheduled Tribes Population by Sex, and Rural/Urban by States 2009-10

STATES	SC			ST		
	MALE	FEMALE	TOTAL	MALE	FEMALE	TOTAL
Andhra Pradesh	61.7	44.6	52.9	56.9	39.2	48.3
Arunachal Pradesh	78.2	75.6	77.1	76.4	67.4	72.1
Assam	89.1	76.3	83.0	84.3	76.6	80.5
Bihar	54.3	29.1	42.5	67.9	45.0	57.0
Chhattisgarh	89.0	72.9	80.9	75.0	58.5	66.9
Goa	100.0	72.1	83.8	98.8	60.0	78.6
Gujrat	74.2	51.3	63.5	74.2	52.7	63.5
Haryana	77.1	52.6	65.6	77.4	42.2	58.9
Himachal Pradesh	84.8	70.9	77.9	81.8	61.4	71.7
Jammu & Kashmir	79.5	63.4	71.7	51.9	18.9	36.5
Jharkhand	66.4	45.5	56.0	64.4	43.0	54.6
Karnataka	65.3	46.7	56.1	65.4	40.6	52.8
Kerala	93.8	81.6	87.6	94.3	82.0	87.0
Madhya Pradesh	78.5	55.2	67.3	65.6	47.8	56.9
Maharashtra	88.2	68.7	78.8	76.3	56.1	66.1
Manipur	87.0	68.0	77.2	90.5	78.8	84.9
Meghalaya	100.0	100.0	100.0	93.8	90.6	92.2

Mizoram	42.1	41.3	41.6	97.8	95.6	96.8
Nagaland	100.0	100.0	100.0	93.8	90.6	92.2
Orissa	74.0	55.8	64.8	62.3	42.5	52.2
Punjab	70.0	56.4	63.7	90.5	84.9	88.0
Rajasthan	69.9	43.6	56.8	66.0	38.0	52.4
Sikkim	90.0	80.9	85.2	89.9	81.9	86.3
Tamil Nadu	75.6	58.7	66.6	55.8	39.2	49.8
Tripura	91,0	78.2	84.7	85.6	70.6	78.5
Uttarakhand	87.6	66.4	76.8	75.8	64.2	69.7
Uttar Pradesh	72.7	46.4	60.0	49.9	38.6	44.1
West Bengal	78.7	62.5	70.9	74.4	57.7	65.8
UNION TERRITORIES						
Andaman & Nicobar	-	-	-	76.9	85.2	80.6
Chandigarh	76.3	92.7	84.8	-	-	-
D & Nagar Haveli	100.0	86.5	92.7	78.4	49.8	65.3
Daman & Diu	100.0	100.0	100.0	99.2	83.9	93.4
Delhi	90.1	60,1	74.0	100.0	-	100.0
Lakshadweep	-	-	-	97.1	88.1	92.5
Pondicherry	80.4	56.0	67.8	-	-	-
INDIA	73.0	52.1	62.8	70.7	52.1	61.6

- Age 7 years and above.

- Source: GOI, NSSO, Primary Data (2009-10).

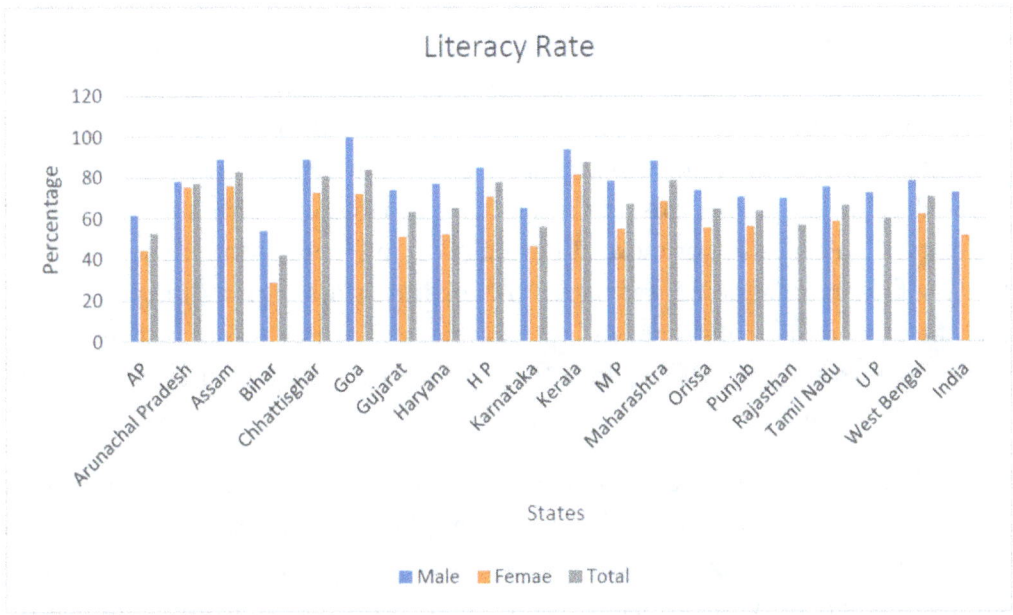

The estimate of unemployment time based on the 25th round of the N.S.S. appears even more disturbing when it is compared with the estimate of time spent in unemployment by the adult male casual agricultural laborers in 1956-57 as shown by the second A.L.E. These data are also presented in Table 15 side-by-side those for the 25th round of the N.S.S. It appears from Table 15 that in 1956-57 the adult male casual agricultural laborers in India were engaged in gainful employment for only 65% of the time and were unemployment for 18.6% of the time. For 16.4% of the time they were not available for gainful work. This is in sharp contrast to the 82% time spent in gainful employment and only 5.7% of the time in unemployment by the adult males in the 'weaker section' (a very comparable group) in 1970-71. Is one to infer from this that there has been a significant increase in the employment available to 'weaker section' of the rural laborer in the 14 years since 1956-57 and a consequent decline in unemployment in their ranks, so much so that rural unemployment had lost it urgency by 1970-71? Before-one comes to any such startling conclusion by a simple comparison of the data from the two surveys, it is prudent to go behind them and look for any differences in concepts and methods that may be responsible for such wide divergence between the two estimates.

Examination of the methods and concepts used in the two surveys reveals a relevant difference in the approach used to measure intensities of time disposition. In the 25th round of N.S.S. the time disposition of each member of the sample household on each of the 7 days preceding the day of enquiry was to be noted. But this was to be noted not in hours but in days. For nothing the intensity of occupation in various activities and intensity of occupation in various activities an intensity code was specified. If the intensity of time disposition on any day was ½ or more, i.e., if a person had spent more than half of this normal working day on any activity, then the intensity was to be recorded as 1. If the intensity was ½ or leas it was to be noted as ½.[3] As against this, the second A.L.E. laid down that a full day's work (intensity 1) will mean ¾ or more of normal working hours. More than ¼ and less than ¾ of the normal hours was taken to constitute work with half intensity. And less than ¼ work has considered as 'normal intensity' which was to be equal to 1/8 of a normal working day. Work done for less than this intensity (i.e., 1/8 day) was to be ignored. The normal working day was taken to be of 10 hours duration.

The difference between the 2nd A.L.E. and the 25th round of N.S.S. in regard to noting the intensity of time disposition might partly at least account for the difference in the findings of the two surveys in their estimation of employment and unemployment. Unfortunately, however, the available tabulated data relating to them do not leave any scope for adjusting one set to conform to the definitions of the other, so that extent of divergence due to this difference in measurements may be broadly indicated.

We may, however, try to get over this difficulty by using the employment data for all rural males from the other N.S.S. rounds. This data are available in a form that permits some maneuverability in regard to the measurement of intensity. Attention may, therefore, be turned to these data. The N.S.S. in the 14th, 15th, 17th and 19th rounds (from 1958 to 1964-65) collected data on employment of the rural population. The tabulated results are made available only for the country. They show the sex-wise division of the rural population into those that were in the labor force and those that were outside it, during the week labor force and those that were outside it, during the week under reference. The information about the detailed activity pattern of the working population during the reference week is presented in two ways. One set of Tables gives the division of the 7 days among various activities like employment, unemployment or not available for work. But since the intensity of each activity is not measured in either the way the A.L.E. or the 25th round set out to measure it, these Tables are not very useful for our purpose. The second set of Tables gives a classification of persons in the rural labor force according to the total number of hours spent by them during the reference week in gainful employment.

These data appear, subject to certain limitations, adjustable for comparison with the employment data given by the 2nd A.L.E. on the one hand and the 25th round of the N.S.S. on the other. We shall set this out in what follows.

Though data on the above lines are available from 4 different N.S.S. rounds for the purpose in hand, it is not necessary to examine them separately, but to take an average of all the four rounds. The differences in the findings of these 4 rounds are not such as to make averaging unhelpful. For purposes of comparison attention shall be contained only to the employment of rural males. The N.S.S. tabulations show (a) the proportion of the total male population in the labor force, (b) the proportion of those in the labor force fully "unemployed" during the week under reference, (c) the proportion of those workers who were gainfully employed for 14 hours or less during the week, (d) the proportion of those employed for more than 14 to 28 hours in the week, (e) the proportion of workers gainfully employed for more than 28 to 42 hours in the week, and (f) the proportion of workers gainfully employed for more than 42 hours in the week.

Now, it is obvious that the male in the labor force according to these N.S.S. rounds are not necessarily the adult males of the 2nd A.L.E. or the males between 15-59 years of age of the 25th round for whom employment data were presented earlier in this study. The 'males in the labor force' might include some non-adults who were gainfully employed for at least one day during the reference week, while it might exclude adult males who were not gainfully employed or were seeking or available for work any time during the week. However, we do not expect this discrepancy between these male populations to create serious differences in estimation of employment in the 3 sets of surveys examined here. The relevant data relating to the rural males from the 4 N.S.S. rounds are summarized in Table 29 below.

Table 33

Pattern of Employment of the Rural Male Labor Force in India (Average of 4 N.S.S. rounds, 14th, 15th, 17th and 19th From 1958 to 1964-65)

A	Proportions of rural males in the labor force	54.87%
B	Out of the total rural males in the labor force (A = 100%), the proportion	
	(i) Unemployed during the week	3.28%
	(ii) Employed for 14 hours or less in the week	5.60%
	(iii) Employed for 15 to 28 hours in the week	7.93%
	(iv) Employed for 29 to 42 hours in the week	15.76%
	(v) Employed for more than 42 hours in the week	65.43

With the help of the above Table, it is possible the estimate the total time spent by the male labor force in gainful employment, by using the alternative measures of intensity of time disposition adopted in the 25th round of the N.S.S. and the 2nd A.L.E. Let us first use the intensity measure of the 25th round of N.S.S. according to its engagement for more than half of a normal working day in any activity will be noted as intensity, that is a full workday and half-a-day or less will be noted as ½ intensity. Now, if a normal working day is considered as of 8 hours duration, then a work week is equal to 56 hours duration. Persons gainfully employed for more than 28 hours may be treated as being fully employed during the week. All those unemployed for 28 hours or less may be considered as employed for only half the week. The rest of the time they as well as those reported as unemployed were either unemployed or were not available for work. Now the N.S.S. rounds do not give estimates of hours for which the workers were not available for work. But we may assume that on an average a rural male worker was not available for work 1/6th of the time (i.e., he was available for work for just over 300 days in a year). This is somewhat higher than the

12.5% time for which the adult male worker (15-59 years of age) was not available for work according to the 25th round. We, however, wish to have a higher estimate since some non-adults are also included in the 4th N.S.S. rounds considered here. Therefore, it can be calculated with the help of the above Table that the rural male labor force was 'unemployed' for about 7% of the time, following broadly the pattern of estimation followed in the 25th round. The estimate thus arrived at is not very different from the 5.7% unemployed time for the adult males among the 'weaker section' in the 25th round.

· Change In The Structure Of Employment

In a study like this we face the almost interactable problem of non-comparability of the Indian census data on working force, which is the consequence of ever-changing concept and definitions. Considering the present employment– unemployment scenario in the country, the Eleventh Five Year Plan strategizes rapid growth in employment opportunities along with improvement in the quality of employment. It recognizes the need to increase the share of regular employment in total employment and a corresponding reduction in casual employment. Attempts to introduce conceptual refinements regarding the definition of 'worker' from census to census. The 1971 census data on working force are more non-comparable with those of the earlier censuses because, for the first time in the history of Indian Census it introduced the concept of 'main activity',[8] to cover full-time workers only. The instruction to enumerators clearly laid down that person engaged in household duties or a studies, who participated in the family economic activity on a less than full time basis, should not be classified as having work as their 'main activity', whereas most of these persons would have been included in the working force under the definition of 1961 census. As a result, the participation rate of workers fell from 42.08 in 1961 to 33.54 in 1971 (the lowest ever recorded in Indian Census) by22% the decrease in the participation rates of females being steeper, 52.86%, from 27.96% in 1961 to13.18 in 1971. Of course, the marginal workers were sought to be netted in the category of 'secondary work' in 1971.While the state wise data on secondary workers engaged in secondary from five percent sample data for the All-India shows that a very small proportion of the non-workers reported some economic activity in 1981. The gap between the work participation rates of males in 1961 and

---

[8]   For criticisma of this criterian see the following:

  (a) J.N.Sinha; "A Rational View of Census Economic Data"

  (b) Srinivasan, K.N., and Sharma. R.N., "on making comparisons of the data of Economically Active Population collected in the census of India, 1961 and 1971;

  (c) Kalra. B.R., "A Preliminary aprisal of 1971 Census Economic Results', paper submitted to the Seminar on First Results of the 1971 Census Of India, Nov., 1971.

1971 tends to close in most States if the 1961 data are so adjusted that workers aged 15 and over in the rural areas, and those in the age group 15-54 in the urban areas, are considered economically active. It is not possible to establish any workable comparability for female workers.

· Inter-Sectoral Changes in Working Force 1961-1971.

We may now study the changes in sectoral distribution of working force during the decade 19611971. Table 4.1 below shows that Kerala, West Bengal, Tamil Nadu, Maharashtra, Gujarat, Punjab and Andhra Pradesh had above India proportion of working force engaged in the non-primary sectors taken to gather in 1961. These States generally had above India proportions separately in the secondary and tertiary sector as well, except that Karnataka too had above India proportion in the secondary sector, while Andhra Pradesh had below India proportion in the tertiary sector.

The only changes since then had been that Karnataka came to have above India proportion in the non-primary sectors taken together. The coefficients of rank correlation between the two rank orders of States in 1961 and 1971 are 0.91 and 0.95 in the primary, secondary and tertiary sector respectively.

Table 34

· Sectoral Distribution of Male Working Forces

STATES	1971				
	PRIMARY SECTOR	SECOND-ARY	SECTOR NON-HOUSEHOLD INDUSTRY	TERTIARY	SECTOR OTHER SERVICES
Andhra Pradesh	69.93	11.94	4.97	18.13	8.54
Assam	76.67	4.89	1.13	18.44	9.65
Bihar	83.45	5.89	2.88	10.57	5.21

Gujarat	65.12	14.85	10.42	20.03	8.78
Jammu & Kashmir	71.13	9.08	3.84	10.79	11.65
Kerala	54.97	6.46	11.19	28.57	12.53
Madhya Pradesh	78.79	8.32	3.75	12.80	7.17
Maharashtra	59.90	17.44	12.53	22.67	10.21
Karnataka	69.83	12.16	6.46	18.01	8.26
Orissa	80.84	6.01	2.33	13.15	8.27
Punjab	65.55	12.44	4.32	22.01	12.11
Rajasthan	75.60	8.33	3.50	16.08	8.83
Tamil Nadu	61.58	15.92	9.99	22.50	9.53
Uttar Pradesh	76.95	8.22	3.91	14.83	8.50
West Bengal	61.76	15.49	11.89	22.75	9.95
All India	70.38	11.32	6.61	18.30	9.08

• **Source: (1) Census Of India, Paper 3 of 1972;** *Economic Characteristics of Population.*

During the decade 1961-71, the proportion of male workers increased in the primary sector, and declined in the secondary and tertiary sectors in the country as a whole and in all the States separately, the only exceptions being Jammu & Kashmir and Maharashtra in each sector, Assam, Kerala and Tamil Nadu in the secondary sector separately and Karnataka in the territory sector above. It may be noted that changes in the proportions in the exception States were very low, except in Jammu & Kashmir. In this connection, we may note two other changes. First, the proportions of male workers employed in the secondary sector declined, or increased slightly, in most of the States, despite an increase in proportions in the non-household industry. Second, the tertiary sector proportions generally declined primarily because of the decline in proportions in another services segment in the tertiary sector, which tends to absorb all the sundry. The implication of these changes is that the increase in the proportions of the primary sector in most of the States has been caused, mainly by a decline in the proportions of workers engaged in the household industry and 'other services'. And this may have meant substitution of one type of unemployment for another.

We now proceed to get further insight from the sectoral distribution of the addition to working force, total and rural, during 1961-1971. Table 5., shows that during the decade!961-71 81.3% of the total increase in male working force (2.97 crores) in the country was absorbed in the primary sector as against 6.6%, in the secondary, and 12.1% in the tertiary sector.

Table 35

- **Number of persons employed per 1000 persons (WFPR0 according to usual status during 1972-73 to 2009-2010**

| ROUND (YEAR) | CATERGORY OF WORKERS | USUALLY EMPLOYED | | | | | | | | |
| | | RURAL | | | URBAN | | | ALL | | |
		MALE	FEMAL	TOTAL	MALE	FEMALE	TOTAL	MALE	FEMALE	TOTAL
66th (2009-10)	PS	537	202	374	539	119	339	538	180	365
	SS only	10	59	34	4	19	11	8	48	27
	All	547	261	408	543	138	350	546	228	392
61th (2004-05)	PS	535	242	391	541	135	346	536	215	380
	SS	11	85	48	8	31	19	11	72	40
	All	546	327	439	549	166	365	547	267	420
55th (1999-2000)	All	531	299	417	518	139	337	527	259	397
50th (1993-1994)	All	553	328	444	521	155	347	545	286	420

43rd (1987-1988)	All	539	323	434	596	152	337	531	285	412
38th (1983)	All	547	340	445	512	151	340	538	296	420
32nd (1978)	All	522	331	444	508	156	341	543	297	423
27th (1973)	All	545	318	*	501	134	*	*	*	*

Ps = principal status, ss= secondary status. proportions not derived for 27th round*

In table 31 the worker-population ratios (WPR's) for two categories of usual status workers viz., (a)usual principal status workers i.e., workers according to usual status (ps) and (b) usual subsidiary status workers i.e., persons working only in a subsidiary status (ss workers). In table above, the WPR's are presented for the years 1977-78, 1983, 1987-88, 1993-94, 1999-2000, and 200910 separately for usual status, secondary status. The two categories together constitute the total usually employed (or all workers) i.e., workers according to the usual status (ps+ss). The first category pertains to those with stable employment. Work Participation Rate figures corresponding to 'all workers' in table 5.1 shows that 55 percent of the male and 23 percent of the females were workers.

Bihar, Orissa, Uttar Pradesh, Kerala, Madhya Pradesh and West Bengal recorded above India absorption of additional working force in primary sector, while Rajasthan and Andhra Pradesh were only slightly short of the National Rate of absorption. It may be noted that all these States except Madhya Pradesh and Rajasthan recorded decline in employment in 'other services' while

only Kerala and west Bengal recorded above India rates of absorption in the secondary sector as well. Bihar and Uttar Pradesh recorded a decline in the working force in the secondary sector during the decade, the former even in the tertiary sector. However, even these States recorded an increase in non-household manufacturing employment. In Jammu & Kashmir, Maharashtra, Karnataka, Tamil Nadu, Gujarat and Punjab the share of the primary sector in the additional working force was below, and that of secondary and tertiary sectors separately above, the national average. All States except Assam and Jammu & Kashmir suffered a decline in employment in household industry, and many States in 'Other Services' too.

As for the addition to rural working force, increase in the male rural working force engaged in the primary sector exceeded the total increase in the rural working force by 3.3% in the country as a whole, the excess being much larger in U P., Bihar, Tamil

Nadu, Orissa, Kerala and West Bengal and almost equal to the All-India average in Gujarat and Madhya Pradesh. In other States, except Assam and Jammu & Kashmir, more than 90% of the additional rural working force was absorbed in the primary sector. While it is possible to have economic development without population transfers from the agriculture to the non-agricultural sector.[9] The possible reverse shift from the more productive urban areas to the less productive rural areas is indicative of acute unemployment situation in the urban areas, which force the marginal rural migrants to go back to the village to share work with their family. Since their already existed considerable volume of unemployment and under-employment in the rural areas the situation would have deteriorated further during the decade.

There is ample evidence to suggest that this has been so, though no firm estimates of rural unemployment are available. The incidence of unemployment in rural India (all ages males) reached the all-time high figure of 11.82. The Planning Commission estimated that rural unemployment increased from about 5.8 million in 1960-61 to about 7 million in 1965-66. The estimated rural unemployment increased from about 5.8 million to about 7 million. The earlier practice of giving estimates of unemployment has been abandoned by the Planning Commission on the recommendations of the committee of experts on unemployment estimates, which was of the view "that estimates of growth in the labor force, of additional employment generated by the plans and of unemployment at the end of the plan periods presented in one dimensional magnitudes are neither meaningful nor useful as indicators of the economic situation"[10] However, this view of the committee has not gone unchallenged. Making use of the NSS data on household consumption, the estimation of poverty of at least 30% of the rural population. Making use of NSS data, the estimation of the number of the wholly unemployed and severely unemployed available for work is about 2.15 million, 1.93 million in the rural areas and 22 lakhs in the urban areas.

The preceding analysis shows that despite an increase of 41% in the net national product and of 13.3% in the per capita income (at 1960-61 prices) during the period 1960-61 to 1970-71 as a result of the public sector expenditure of about Rs. 20,000 crores during the decade, the pressure of population on agriculture and allied industries has increased. Thus, changes in the industrial distribution of working force seem to run counter to the Clark fisher hypothesis that ".....as time goes on and communities become more economically advanced, the numbers engaged in agricultural tend to decline relative to the numbers engaged in services"[11] They further show that the planners took a very

9   Khusro .A.m., Economic Development with No Population Transfers, Institute of Economic Growth, Occasional paper No. 4.

10 Planning Commision : Reports of the Committee of Experts on Unemployment Estimates. p.31.

11 Clark. Colin: Conditions of Economic Progress.

optimistic view of the prospect of growth of national income and population. It was thought on the eve of second plan that the projected relative decline of the proportion employed in agriculture by about 13% while the national income goes up by 100% would be in keeping with the historical experience in other countries.

We estimate the incidence of rural poverty across all three social groups, and relate this to their demographic, educational and occupational characteristics. An important issue that we need to address in determining the poverty status of households is the choice of the poverty line.

Table. 36

- **Sectoral Distribution of increase in Male Working Force 196–71**

SECONDARY SECTOR					
STATES	PRIMARY SECTOR	HOUSEHOLD INDUSTRY	NON HOUSEHOLD INDUSTRY	CONCENTRATED	TOTAL
Andhra Pradesh	80.2	-9.3	10.1	2.9	3.7
Assam	77.4	2.5	2.9	0.5	5.9
Bihar	106.5	-4.3	2.2	-0.1	-2.2
Gujarat	74.2	-5.7	14.2	1.9	10.4
Jammu & Kashmir	53.2	4.9	3.4	8.1	16.4
Kerala	90.7	-3.3	16.5	4.0	17.2
Madhya Pradesh	87.4	-2.9	6.0	-1.2	1.9
Maharashtra	56.5	-3.1	19.8	2.0	18.7
Karnataka	71.3	-3.0	10.8	0.7	8.5

Orissa	97.3	-4.4	6.0	0.6	2.2
Punjab	79.3	-7.4	9.0	1.5	3.1
Rajasthan	81.1	-3.8	6.7	0.2	3.1
Tamil Nadu	71.4	-5.5	20.4	1.7	16.6
Uttar Pradesh	96.9	-7.5	6.7	-1.0	-1.8
West Bengal	84.3	0.8	8.3	-1.0	7.9
All India	81.3	-4.5	10.1	0.9	6.6

An alternative measures of the rate of unemployment, which is an average of the different weekly situations over the whole year during which the survey was conducted has been obtained from the data on activity, particulars collected for all the individuals of the households. In the past, the measure was interpreted as the percentage of the number of unemployed persons to the total population. But this rate should better be termed as the measure of the level of unemployment (or underutilization) of the manpower resources, as in the words of the committee of experts, "it is inappropriate to assume that the percentage of unemployed during a round- based on data collected over a year, refers to full-time unemployment because persons who may be without work and seeking or available for work during the reference period of one week may not be without work throughout the year." In this study, the rate or level of unemployment, estimated on the basis of classification of individuals by current activity status as obtained in varying reference weeks has been expressed as a percentage of unemployed person-weeks and not as the percentage of the number of unemployed persons.

Table.37

· **Sectoral Distribution of Increase in Male Working force 1971**

STATES	TRADE AND COMMERCE	TERTIARY SECTOR		TOTAL	INCREASE IN RURAL WORKERS
		TRANSPORT	OTHER SERVICES		

Andhra Pradesh	10.9	5.6	-0.4	16.1	98.5
Assam	9.4	4.4	3.0	16.8	55.2
Bihar	4.4	1.1	-9.3	-4.2	115.2
Gujarat	11.2	4.5	-0.03	15.4	103.0
Jammu & Kashmir	10.9	11.9	7.6	30.4	64.7
Kerala	26.4	9.1	-43.4	-7.9	107.2
Madhya Pradesh	5.5	2.1	3.1	10.7	102.8
Maharashtra	15.4	4.3	5.1	24.8	90.0
Karnataka	13.5	8.2	-1.5	20.2	82.0
Orissa	8.1	3.8	11.4	0.5	108.5
Punjab	8.7	2.5	6.3	17.5	92.1
Rajasthan	6.0	2.8	6.9	15.7	97.2
Tamil Nadu	19.7	8.9	-16.8	12.0	111.0
Uttar Pradesh	4.6	2.3	-2.0	4.9	118.8
West Bengal	8.6	6.7	-7.5	7.8	104.9
All India	10.3	4.6	-2.8	12.1	103.3

The number of unemployed person weeks based on classification of persons by current activity status, would be 5.78 lakhs- 4.18 lakhs in rural areas and 1.60 lakhs in urban areas. It is seen that the rates in both for rural and urban areas and for males and females in the State are much higher than the corresponding rates obtained from the classification of individuals by usual activity status. The hypothesis postulated by the Expert Committee that, in the main, persons who may be without work and seeking work or available for work during the reference week may not be without work throughout the year has thus been borne out by the findings of the survey despite the fact that in a few cases persons reporting as usually unemployed were found to be employed in the 'current week'.

Table-38

· Duration of Endeavour to Get Employment (Percent)

RURAL					
1. Percentage to total persons			0.59	0.16	0.38
2. Since when seeking or Available for employment:	(a) Up to One Year		57.34	22.82	48.65
	(b) One Year and above		42.66	77.18	51.35
URBAN					
1. Percentage to total (population) persons			2.93	0.86	1.98
2. Since when seeking or available for employment:	(a) Up to One Year		37.46	67.52	43.68
	(b) One Year and above		62.54	32.48	56.32

Though the large gap in poverty rates between Scheduled and non-Scheduled groups may not be surprising, it is important to understand what causes the poverty gap between the scheduled and non-scheduled groups to be so large.

Table-39

· Percentage of Unemployed Person-weeks

	MALE	FEMALE	TOTAL
Rural	1.79	2.50	2.13
Urban	3.80	1.16	2.52

There is no need to be disturbed by this apparently contradictory situation as whatever little work they had during the week was not worthwhile to be considered as substantive employment and therefore, they preferred as usually unemployed. The estimates of the unemployed person-weeks has two components: One is mainly the average of the unemployed weeks of persons otherwise classified as usually "seeking and available" (categorized as chronically unemployed here) and the other is the average of the unemployed weeks of persons classified as "working". If the first component, i.e., the contribution of the chronically unemployed persons (seeking and available) is taken out from the total pool of the unemployed persons-weeks, the residual is essentially an estimate of the average level of under-employment of the persons otherwise classified as usually 'working.'

A quantitative measure of the rate of under-employment can thus be derived as the percentage of number of under-employed persons to the total population. Applying this rate to the appropriate projected population; we get the total estimates of the under-employed persons it is 3.80 lakhs- 3.43 lakhs in rural areas and 0.37 lakhs in urban areas. Comparing the respective estimates of persons usually seeking and available (Table 38) and persons-weeks seeking and available (Table 39) we can locate the rate of under-employment. The comparative position of the percentage of seeking and available person-weeks for all the States and for all India is shown in Table-XV.

It is seen that the under-employment rate is higher in Karnataka State than all India average; it is very high in Kerala, Andhra Pradesh, Jammu & Kashmir, it is also high in Bihar, Orissa and Tamil Nadu.

Table 40

- ### Percentage of seeking and Available for Work Person Week by Current Activity Status

SL. NO.	STATES	RURAL			URBAN		
		MALE	FEMALE	TOTAL	MALE	FEMALE	TOTAL
1.	Andhra Pradesh	2.02	3.97	2.98	4.74	2.52	3.58
2.	Assam	0.82	0.19	0.53	1.36	0.27	0.90
3.	Bihar	2.46	1.82	2.16	3.58	1.02	2.42
4.	Gujarat	1.30	0.87	1.11	2.11	0.37	1.28
5.	Haryana	1.20	0.25	0.75	3.20	1.07	2.26

6.	Jammu Kashmir	8.84	0.64	4.78	2.66	0.64	1.68
7.	Karnataka	1.79	2.50	2.13	3.80	1.16	2.52
8.	Kerala	6.04	4.35	5.16	8.17	4.20	6.15
9.	Madhya Predesh	0.88	1.20	1.06	2.00	0.80	1.46
10.	Maharashtra	1.65	1.76	1.70	3.33	1.55	2.53
11.	Orissa	2.13	2.50	2.30	2.77	1.55	2.22
12.	Punjab	1.28	0.32	0.84	2.58	1.35	2.02
13.	Rajasthan	3.22	1.89	2.58	2.43	.082	1.67
14.	Tamil Nadu	2.36	1.65	2.01	4.43	1.72	3.09
15.	Uttar Pradesh	0.89	0.69	0.80	1.67	0.27	1.04
16.	West Bengal	1.66	1.28	1.46	5.16	1.71	3.68
	All India	1.86	1.73	1.80	3.38	1.40	2.45

• Source: N.S.S., op. Cit, p. 20.

The rate of unemployment (or under-employment) expressed in terms of unemployed persons-weeks estimated separately for different seasons or sub-rounds may also indicate the level of seasonal unemployment as it is commonly know that in the case of self-employed (particularly in rural agricultural and non-agricultural enterprises and to some extent, in urban areas as well) the seasonal fluctuations in work and employment is a factor to be reckoned with. The rate of unemployment given here gives only a conservative estimate of the level of unemployment (or underemployment). For the large towns or cities, where the pattern of unemployment is more organized and self-employment in agricultural enterprise play a dominant role compared to that in rural areas, seasonality is much less and the weekly work pattern of individuals recorded in the survey is not likely to vary widely as they do in rural areas. Under these circumstances, the level of unemployed expressed as unemployed person-weeks can, perhaps, also be interpreted as number of persons unemployed. This means that the number of persons unemployed in urban areas of Karnataka was 1.60 lakhs in 1972-73. On the basis of the data furnished by the employment exchanges in the State, the total number of candidates on the live register was 293,186. The employment exchange data was being used for estimating the unemployment in the urban areas. But the data on the number of persons on the live register do not permit reliable estimates of the volume of urban unemloyment because (a) some of the registered candidates are not part of urban unemployed and they may be residing in rural areas; (b) some of them may be in employment but still keeping their names on the register and some others who have registered are students; and (c) some of the urban unemployed have registered at more than one exchange. Thus, these two sets of data on urban unemployment are basically non-comparable.

The third measure of the rate of unemployment (or under-employment) in terms of the total number of recorded days of seeking or available for work of persons in a week expressed as percentage of the total number of days on which the household members report themselves to be in the labor force (i.e., report either working or and available for work) during the different weeks of the particular sub-round of the survey has also been obtained. This measure will bring out the proportion of the days seeking or available of the total labor force days, on the average during the period of survey indicating the extent of underutilization of the available labor supply. It is necessary, however, to use this data cautiously and it will not be correct to interpret this figure as the estimate of the number of people who remained unemployed.

Table 41

- **Percentage of Person days Seeking and Available of the Total Labor Force Person-weeks**

	MALE	FEMALE	TOTAL
Rural	7.40	11.62	9.04
Urban	8.41	7.67	7.64

The percentage of person-days seeking and available of the total labor force persons-days in a week is shown in the table. The rate is quite high in the rural areas and moderately high in urban areas. The All-India picture is presented in Table below. The rate is quite high in the rural areas and moderately high in urban areas. The all-India picture is presented in the Table above. It is seen that the rate is very high in the rural areas of Kerala, Bihar, Tamil Nadu, West Bengal, Andhra Predesh and Orissa. In the urban areas, it is very high in Kerala, Andhra Pradesh, Rajasthan and West Bengal. According to a study based on an analysis of 2011 Census data and research studies by India Migration Now, a Mumbai-based non-profit, poverty and lack of opportunity forced 93 million Indians from disadvantaged castes and tribes to migrate to other areas within their states in the hope of securing education or employment. However, social segregation, labour market discrimination and barriers to accessing the most basic services continued to plague their livelihood and everyday life, revealed the study.

Table 42

• Percentage of Persons-days Seeking and available to Total Labour Force Persons- days in a Week

SL. NO	STATES	RURAL			URBAN		
		Male	Female	Total	Male	Female	Total
1	Andhra Pradesh	6.43	14.72	9.61	10.88	16.89	12.47
2	Assam	2.23	2.42	2.25	3.28	5.26	3.42
3	Bihar	8.85	13.83	10.17	7.62	14.00	8.48
4	Gujarat	6.42	5.51	6.08	6.54	5.50	6.34
5	Haryana	3.33	1.06	2.52	7.65	11.68	8.16
6	Jammu & Kashmir	17.17	5.39	14.36	5.90	11.52	6.56
7	Karnataka	7.40	11.62	9.04	8.41	7.67	7.64
8	Kerala	22.96	26.76	24.26	22.99	24.10	23.23
9	Madhya Pradesh	2.38	3.83	2.98	4.11	6.35	4.61
10	Maharashtra	7.21	10.53	8.64	7.48	12.44	8.43
11	Orissa	7.06	14.84	9.32	5.76	13.12	7.15
12	Punjab	4.40	1.87	3.67	5.96	8.91	6.46
13	Rajastan	5.32	3.24	4.41	5.11	4.55	5.02

14	Tamil Nadu	9.38	12.56	10.63	9.78	14.29	10.84
15	Uttar Pradesh	2.98	3.37	3.11	4.34	3.31	4.19
16	West Bengal	8.45	14.52	9.55	9.62	17.32	10.52
	All-India	6.57	9.20	7.48	7.70	12.03	8.53

• **Source: N.S.S., *op.,cit.,* p.22.**

CHAPTER VII

MIGRATION IN INDIA

<u>Migration</u> is the movement of people in space, often involving a change in the usual place of residence; internal migration is such a movement within national boundaries where people leave their native place to move to nearby towns and cities or places of better opportunities in a hope to improve their livelihoods. In India, according to the <u>Economic Survey of India 2017</u> estimates the magnitude of inter-state migration was close to 9 million annually between 2011 and 2016, while Census 2011 revealed that total number of internal migrants in the country (accounting for inter- and intra-state movement) was at a staggering 139 million. Uttar Pradesh and Bihar were the biggest source states, followed closely by Madhya Pradesh, Punjab, Rajasthan, Uttarakhand, Jammu and Kashmir and West Bengal; the major destination states are Delhi, Maharashtra, Tamil Nadu, Gujarat, Andhra Pradesh and Kerala. Moreover, as per <u>data from Census 2011</u>, about 16% of the total intra-state migrants in India belonged to the SCs and 8% to the STs, almost equal to their share in the total population. This proportion had remained constant since 2001, when SCs made up 15.7% and STs 8% of intra-state migrants.

Migration in India– Benefits and Challenges

In August 2019, an India Spend <u>report</u> had highlighted that ***internal migration***, both within a state and across states in India, had the potential to improve households' socio-economic status, and benefit both the region that people migrate to and where they migrate from. Despite this, the research also showed, scheduled castes (SC)– castes considered 'lower' in the social hierarchy– and scheduled tribes (ST) indigenous tribal populations– benefited less from migration as social discrimination continued to impact them in the places they migrated to. Moreover, exclusionary government policies often push migrants, from all social groups, to the fringes of cities that have limited civic infrastructure and municipal facilities, which makes migrants prone to poor health and living conditions, as India Spend reported in October 2019.

The impact of such policies on migrants from the SCs and STs was greater, as those belonging to these groups are also some of the poorest in the country, showed an analysis of data from the government's national sample survey on expenditure in 2011-12, published in the Journal of Social Inclusion Studies. For instance, when migrants move away from their hometowns, they can no longer access the benefits of state-specific schemes such as the public distribution system. This impacts the poorest and food-insecure the most. Those from the scheduled castes and tribes cannot avail of reservations–which try to correct historical discrimination against these groups - in state government jobs and state-run educational institutions when they migrate from one state to another, the Supreme Court ruled in 2018.

How caste impacted decision to migrate: Whether migration leads to accumulation of wealth or not was also influenced by caste, networks, and land possessed, concluded a 2016 study from Beed in Maharashtra, published in the Social Science Spectrum. Families that were only seasonally involved in sugarcane cutting were better off than those involved in the job permanently, the study found. Also, there were overlaps between a migrant's social and economic status. People from the general category and Other Backward Classes (OBC) had higher chances of migrating and bearing the cost of migration. The disadvantaged castes were often unable to gain the benefits of migration. Migration played off if the worker was from a higher caste, found a 2018 study linking caste and job market participation among migrants in the slum areas of four Indian cities– Ludhiana, Ujjain, Mathura and Jaipur.

· Labor market and social segregation

A 2018 study in southern Rajasthan by the Aajeevika Bureau, published in the Journal of Interdisciplinary Economics, had found that communities that have been historically at the lower end of social groups were also the most disadvantaged in the labor market. Over 79% of the migration (mostly men) in the study was inter-state, with Gujarat as the most popular destination. At the destination, the work was disaggregated based on caste, leaving STs no choice but to work at the lowest end of the labor market. Among ST migrants, more than half worked as helpers and about 30% worked as masons, the study found. Other migrants from the 'general' category and OBCs performed more skilled tasks. Migrants from the 'general' category had better qualifications for urban job centers, because of the historical advantage of education and are therefore able to find higher-paying jobs in urban areas.

Caste and Women Migrants

Women from SCs and STs often migrate from one rural area to the other because of displacement and loss in the ownership of forest resources, a 2012 study on gender and migration, conducted across 20 states of India by the Centre for Women's Development Studies, Delhi between 2008 and 2011 showed. Even here, caste played a decisive factor among women in deciding the nature of employment and the nature of migration. Most tribal women were concentrated in the construction sector, lower-caste women in sectors such as brickmaking, and OBC migrant women worked as paid domestic workers and seasonal agricultural workers, according to the report.

Of a sample of 1,600 families surveyed in four states, more than three-fourths of migrant tribal women from Chhattisgarh, Jharkhand and Odisha worked as domestic servants while migrant tribal women from Madhya Pradesh were engaged in wage employment, found a 2010 report by the Society for Regional Research and Analysis. The report also found that long-and medium-term female migration was dominated by migrants from the 'general' category, while most tribal women migrated for the short or medium term.

Caste and Emigration

Since the 1970s, when Kerala had high unemployment, it became lucrative to move to the Gulf region to fill the surge in demand for skilled and unskilled labor. However, SC/ST community emigration reduced in Kerala, found eight rounds of the Kerala Migration Survey, conducted by the Centre for Development Studies in Trivandrum. In 1998, 1.4% of emigrants were from the SC/ST community which reduced to 0.9% in the 2018 survey. The low SC/ST emigration deepens caste inequalities as remittances play a crucial role in Kerala's economy and the prosperity of its population, according to a 2017 study published in Routledge India. Even when those from the lower castes emigrate, they face discrimination. As many as a quarter (26%) of 1,500 Dalits from South Asia interviewed in the United States of America had faced physical violence because of their caste, while 20% reported discrimination at their workplaces, according to a survey conducted in 2016 by Equality Labs, a US-based research organization.

The survey also found that 40% of the respondents were made to feel unwelcome at their place of worship, 40% said they were rejected as romantic partners because of their caste and 60% had experienced caste-based derogatory jokes and comments. It was tougher for female emigrants, who often face violence and abuse at destination countries and are unable to reach out for help as many are isolated as domestic workers in households, said Sister Lissy, the founder of the National Workers Movement, a Hyderabad-based nongovernmental organization that works for the welfare of female emigrants.

· An Overview of Poverty by Caste

The Scheduled Caste constitutes a significant demographic strength in India. Most of India's poor live in rural areas. Our focus is on rural poverty. Most of India's poor live in rural areas.

Table 43

· Literacy Rates for Total and Backward Caste by Sex- 2001

STATES/UT	PROPORTION OF SC & ST POPULATION		LITERACY RATE OF SC & ST POPULATION	
	SC	ST	SC	ST
INDIA	16.2	8.2	54.69	47.10
Jammu & Kashmir	7.6	10.9	59.03	37.46
Himachal Pradesh	24.7	4.0	70.31	65.50
Punjab	28.9	-	56.22	-
Chandigarh	17.5	-	67.66	-
Uttaranchal	17.9	3.0	63.40	63.23
Haryana	19.3	-	55.45	-

Delhi	16.9	-	70.85	-
Rajasthan	17.2	12.6	52.24	44.66
Uttar Pradesh	21.1	0.1	46.27	35.13
Bihar	15.7	0.9	28.47	28.17
Sikkim	5.0	20.6	63.04	67.14
Arunachal Predesh	0.6	64.2	67.64	49.62
Nagaland	-	89.1	-	65.95
Manipur	2.8	34.2	72.32	65.85
Mizoram	-	94.5	89.20	89.34
Tripura	17.4	31.1	74.68	56.48
Meghalaya	0.5	85.9	56.27	61.34
Assam	6.9	12.4	66.78	62.52
West Bengal	23.0	5.5	59.04	43.40
Jharkand	11.8	26.3	37.56	40.67
Orissa	16.5	22.1	55.53	37.37
Chhattisghar	11.6	31.8	63.96	52.09
Madhaya Pradesh	15.2	20.3	58.57	41.16
Gujarat	7.1	14.8	70.50	47.74
Daman & Diu	3.1	8.8	85.13	63.42
Dadar & Nagar Havali	1.9	62.2	78.25	41.24
Maharastra	10.2	8.9	71.90	55.21
Andra Pradesh	16.2	6.6	53.52	37.04

Karnataka	16.2	6.6	52.87	48.27
Gao	1.8	-	71.92	55.88
Lakshadweep	-	94.5	-	86.14
Kerala	9.8	1.1	82.66	64.35
Tamil Nadu	19.0	1.0	63.19	41.53
Pondicherry	16.2	0.0	69.12	-
Andaman & Nicobar Island	0.0	8.3	-	66.79

• *Source: Government Of India (2006)*

The caste-based ideology of hereditary occupations prescribes the most minimal and lowly of occupations to SC groups and has determined the socio-economic life of these communities. While SC's have traditionally been denied education, even those with education have experienced very limited social mobility due to caste-based opposition to their occupational mobility (Jeffercy ct., al. 2002). On the other hand, the Scheduled Tribes belong to different sets of economic and cultural factors that have little to do with caste ideology. Scheduled Tribes has isolated from mainstream of Indian society. This has afforded them a measure of cultural autonomy and economic independence. Modernization and accumulative processes of production have resulted in massive encroachment into their natural habits. This has in turn resulted in displacement, poverty and heightened levels of exploitation through a system of 'boded labor'. The histories of exploitation and marginalization of Scheduled Caste and Scheduled Tribe communities have produced different engagements with education as a path to social mobility.

According to the 2001 census, the ST population is 84,326,240 and constitutes 8.2 percent of the total population of India. This population grew by 24.5% during the period 1991-2001 (Census Of India, 2002). The SC population on the other hand, is 166,635,700 and constitutes 16.2 percent of the total population of India. The cultural marginalization and oppression faced by Scheduled Caste and Scheduled Tribes that mainstream education is its inability to deliver the promise of jobs and upward economic mobility. In the experience of Scheduled Caste and Scheduled Tribes, therefore, failure to get a job in the modern economy means a double loss, because the 'educated' child is ill-equipped and/or unwilling to participate in the economic activity of the household. The reluctance of SC and ST parents to keep their children in school can be traced to the disconnection between school education and their prospects in the economy. The discontent with schooling as a path towards social and economic mobility is only likely to increase among Scheduled Caste and Scheduled Tribes with the growth in the casualization of the labor force in urban and rural sector, a phenomenon that started in the 1990's with economic liberalization reforms.

Recent studies show that there is an increased demand for education among Scheduled Caste and Scheduled Tribes (M Sedwal, 2008). A little over 73 percent of the households belonged to rural India and accounted for nearly 75 percent of total population. About 9 percent of the households in the country belonged to *scheduled tribes* (ST), about 20 percent belonged to *scheduled caste* (SC) and about 40 percent belonged to the *other backward class* (OBC). About 8 percent, 20 percent and 41 percent of the Indian population belonged to the categories ST, SC, and OBC. The proportion of persons belonging to the categories ST, SC and OBC were about 11 percent, 22 percent and 42 percent, respectively in the rural areas and about 3 percent, 15 percent and 36 percent, respectively in the urban areas.

We thus see that the child sex ratio patterns among the scheduled castes have tended to follow the pattern among the 'general' or the other castes rather than those among the scheduled tribes. Thus, clubbing the two groups together, as is traditionally done in the policy as well as academic circles is inappropriate. Second, the role of the 'region' seems to be more significant than the factor of being the part of 'scheduled castes. Table below presents an interesting statistic on the f/m ratio among the 0-4 and 5-9 age group by the% of the SC population in three group of districts with low (<10%), medium (10-20%) and high (>20%) percentage of the SC population. Among districts with low, moderate and high concentration of the Scheduled caste population one could notice lowering of FMR 5-9 among the districts where scheduled caste population has moderate or high concentration. A further indication perhaps that in such districts the scheduled

We thus see that the child sex ratio patterns among the scheduled castes have tended to castes start behaving 'more like the higher castes than they used to be' as described by Dreze and Sen (1995) for the SC population in UP. Goody and Berreman in their persuasive analyses have already drawn attention towards female subordination being a 'precondition' of upward social mobility a point further amplified by Vishwanath (2004) more recently in the context of the analysis of the female infanticide during the colonial rule. If the scheduled castes follow the same female- regressive social make up that has characterized the landowning and hypergamous upper castes, the cancer of female feticide is bound to spread among them. Given the process of 'Sanskritization' they are subject to this is inevitable unless social reform accompanies their upward mobility. Higher female workforce participation which had earlier characterized the scheduled castes may come down in the wake of prosperity for the sake of 'status production' (Papanek, 1989). The SC female children may then face the double burden; Sanskritization on one hand and reduced economic worth on the other. Extricating them from the 'twin danger' is a challenge for society indeed! scheduled tribes. Thus, clubbing the two groups together, as is traditionally done in the policy as well as academic circles is inappropriate. Second, the role of the 'region' seems to be more significant than the factor of being the part of 'scheduled castes. Table below presents an interesting statistic on the f/m ratio among the 0-4 and 5-9 age group by the% of the SC population in three group of districts with low (<10%), medium (10-20%) and high (>20%) percentage of the SC population. Among districts with low, moderate and high concentration of the Scheduled caste population one could notice lowering of FMR 5-9 among the districts where scheduled caste population has moderate or high concentration.

During 2004-2005, the household size in the rural areas was the lowest among the ST's (4.6). In the urban areas, it was lowest for both ST's and others (4.3) each. During the same period, the overall sex ratio in India was 951 females per 1000 males. The sex ratio was 959 among the ST's 954 for both the SC's and OBC's, and 943 among others. In rural India, proportion of households depending on self-employment was higher among the other category of households (61 percent) or among OBC category of households (56 percent) as compared to that among the ST (46 precent) or SC (34 percent) households. In urban India too, proportion of households depending on self-employment was higher among the OBC households (40 percent) and others category ring 2004-2005, the household size in the rural areas was the lowest among the ST's (4.6). In the urban areas, it was the lowest for bothering 2004-2005, the household size in the rural areas was the lowest among the ST's (4.6). In the urban areas, it was the lowest for bothering 2004-2005, the household size in the rural areas was the lowest among the ST's (4.6). In the urban areas, it was lowest for both ST's and others (4.3) each. During the same period, the overall sex ratio in India was 951 females per 1000 males. The sex ratio was 959 among the ST's 954 for both the SC's and OBC's, and 943 mongering 2004-2005, the household size in the rural areas was the lowest among the ST's (4.6). In the urban areas, it was lowest for both ST's and others (4.3) each. During the same period, the overall sex ratio in India was 951 females per 1000 males. The sex ratio was 959 among the ST's 954 for both the SC's and OBC's, and 943 among others. In rural India, proportion of households depending on self-employment was higher among the other category of households (61 percent) or others. In rural India, proportion of households depending on self-employment was higher among the other category of households (61 percent) or ST's and others (4.3) each. During the same period, the overall sex ratio in India was 951 females per 1000 males. The sex ratio was 959 among the ST's 954 for both the SC's and OBC's, and 943 among others.

In rural India, proportion of households depending on self-employment was higher among the other category of households (61 percent) or ST's and others (4.3) each. During the same period, the overall sex ratio in India was 951 females per 1000 males. The sex ratio was 959 among the ST's 954 for both the SC's and OBC's, and 943 among others. In rural India, proportion of households depending on self-employment was higher among the other category of households (61 percent) or households (39 precent) as compared to that among the ST (26 percent) or SC (29 percent) households. In the rural areas, the proportion of households in the highest monthly per-capita consumer expenditure (MPCE) class (i.e., those who spent Rs. 1155 or more per month) was higher among other categories of households (12 percent) than among the OBC's (5 percent), SC's (3 percent) or ST's (2 percent). The proportion of urban households in the highest MPCE class (I.e., those who spent Rs. 2540 or more per month) was higher among other (13 percent) category of households than among the OBC's or ST's (3 percent each) or SC's (1 percent).

About 26 percent of the households in the rural areas and 8 percent in the urban areas had no literate members of age 15 years and above. The proportion of households without any literate adult (15 years and above) member or without any literate adult female member was much higher among the households belonging to the ST's and SCs compared to the OBC's or other category households in both rural and urban India. In the rural areas, for every 1000 households, about 17 households reported that at least one male member had got the work in public works, whereas only 8 households reported that at least one female member had got the work in public works for at least 60 days during the previous 365 days. Among the social groups, the incidence is found to be higher for the ST's followed by the SC's and OBC's.

About 34 percent people of India were literate. The literacy rate was the highest among the others (78 percent) category of people, followed by the OBC's with a gap of nearly 13 percentage points, and the lowest among the ST's (52 percent). According to the usual status, about 56 percent of rural males and 33 percent of rural females belonged to the labor force. The corresponding proportions in the urban areas were 57 percent and 18 percent, respectively.

According to the usual status, about 42 percent of the population in the country was usually employed. The proportion was 44 percent in the rural and 37 percent in the urban. About 55 percent of rural males and 33 percent of rural female were employed. The corresponding proportion in the urban areas were 55 percent and 17 percent, respectively. The Worker Proportion Ratio (WPR) according to the usual status, was the highest among the males (56 percent) and females (44 percent) belonging to the ST's (50 percent). In urban India, however, the proportion of person employed was the same among SC and ST workers (38 percent each) and was about 35 percent among others. Among the rural males WPR was higher for persons belonging to ST's (89 percent) and SC's (86 percent) than that for OBC's (85 percent) and other (82 percent).

In the rural areas, among both males and females, the proportion of chronically unemployed was the highest for the other category of persons. Between the two categories of ST's and SC's rural households, proportion of chronically unemployed among the males and females was higher among the SC's than among the ST's. Among the urban males, the proportion of chronically unemployed was the highest among SC's followed by that among the other categories. For urban females, the proportion of chronically unemployed was slightly lower for SC's and ST's than for those belong to the OBC's or another category.

When we look poverty at the State and National Level, the most wonderful fact is that the poverty ratio of these States which participate the most in the economic reform process such as Maharashtra, Tamil Nadu, Karnataka, Madhya Pradesh, West Bengal have more poverty ration than that States which participated least such as Kerala, Punjab, Haryana, Rajasthan, etc. So, it is evident that no certain and positive relationship between economic reform and poverty elimination. As far as the matter of poverty reduction is concerned, the poor people must be provided meaningful employment and the availability of essential goods for their lives and livelihood.

Table 44

· POVERTY RATIO OF DIFFERENT STATES OF INDIA

STATES/ YEAR	1987-1988		1993-1994		1999-2000	
	RURAL	URBAN	RURAL	URBAN	RURAL	URBAN
Jammu & Kashmir	25.70	17.47	30.34	9.18	3.97	1.98
Punjab	12.60	14.67	11.95	11.35	6.35	5.75
Himachal Pradesh	16.28	6.29	30.34	9.18	7.94	4.63

Haryana	16.22	17.99	28.02	16.38	8.27	9.99
Kerala	29.10	40.33	25.76	24.55	9.38	20.27
Gujarat	28.67	37.26	22.18	27.89	13.17	15.59
Rajasthan	33.21	41.92	26.46	30.49	13.74	19.85
Andhra Pradesh	20.92	40.11	15.92	38.33	10.05	26.63
Mizoram	39.35	9.94	45.01	7.73	40.04	7.47
Karnataka	32.89	48.12	29.88	40.14	17.38	25.25
Tamil Nadu	45.80	38.64	32.48	22.14	20.55	22.11
Maharashtra	40.78	39.78	37.93	35.15	23.72	26.81
West Bengal	48.30	35.08	40.80	22.41	31.85	14.86
Manipur	39.35	9.94	45.01	7.73	40.04	7.47
Uttar Pradesh	14.10	42.96	42.28	35.59	31.22	30.89
Nagaland	39.35	9.94	45.01	7.73	40.04	7.74
Arunachal Pradesh	39.35	9.94	45.01	7.73	40.04	7.47
Meghalaya	39.35	9.94	45.01	7.73	40.04	7.47
Tripura	39.35	9.94	45.01	7.73	40.04	7.47
Assam	39.35	9.94	45.01	7.73	40.04	7.47
Sikkim	39.34	9.94	45.01	7.73	40.04	7.47
Madhya Pradesh	41.92	47.09	40.64	48.38	37.06	38.44
Bihar	52.63	48.73	58.21	34.50	44.30	32.91

Orissa	57.64	41.63	49.72	41.64	48.01	42.83
All India	39.09	38.20	37.27	32.36	27.09	23.62

- Source: Planning Commission, Five-year plan (2002-2007), Govt. of India.

Poverty is essentially a problem of low/ almost nil productivity of the poor. These people either do not produce or produce very little, so that their income remains low for a level of consumption- experience can lift them above their miserable living. The problem of poverty and unemployment is considered as a biggest challenge to development planning in India. High poverty levels are synonymous with poor quality of life. About 320 million people of India live below poverty line in 1993-94. This constitutes as such as 35.97% of the total population of the country.

The poor in the rural areas are 37.27% of the rural population. Those in the urban areas account for 32.36% of the urban population. Unemployment simply means a situation when able and willing people are not getting jobs as per their own capabilities. Unemployment in India is structural in nature, i.e., productive capacity is inadequate to create a sufficient number of jobs. This is a chronic phenomenon.

It is true that economic growth creates opportunities of employment. Rural unemployed were ignored in comparison with urban unemployed persons. As a result, rural unemployed are running towards the urban areas. If this acute problem of unemployment is not solved, then there will be an explosive situation in future.

Table 45

· PAST AND PRESENT EMPLOYMENT AND UNEMPLOYMENT SCENARIO

	MILLION			GROWTH PER ANNUM	
	1983	1993-1994	1999-2000	1993-1994	1993-2000
ALL INDIA					
Population	718.20	894.01	1003.93	2.00	1.95

Labor Force	261.33	335.97	363.33	2.43	1.31
Unemployment Rate (%)	(8.30)	(5.99)	(7.32)	-	-
No. of unemployed	21.76	20.13	26.38	-0.08	4.74
Rural					
Population	546.61	658.83	727.50	1.79	1.67
Labor Force	204.18	255.38	270.89	2.15	0.96
Workforce	187.92	241.04	250.89	2.40	0.67
Unemployment Rate (%)	(7.96)	(5.61)	(7.21)		
No. Of unemployed	16.26	14.34	19.50	-1.19	5.26
Urban					
Population	171.59	234.98	276.47	3.04	2.74
Labor Force	57.15	89.60	92.95	3.33	2.40
Workforce	51.64	74.80	85.84	3.59	2.32
Unemployment rate (%)	(9.64)	(7.19)	(7.65)		
No. of unemployed	5.51	5.80	7.11	0.49	3.45

• **Source: Planning Commission.**

As the economic reform took place in India, the number of forces causing unemployment increased and thus increasing, the number of poor and hence the problem of poverty. Unemployment is the outcome of this gigantic development and poverty is the progeny of progress. About 260.2 million people in India, living below the poverty line.

Dimensions of Under-Employment

A study on the nature and dimension of under-employment can only be meaningful and relevent if the necessary background information on the usual work pattern of the population is made available. From the data collected in the NSS 27th round survey we get the distribution of population by detailed usual activity status category, separately for areas rural and urban and also for males and females. This distribution will reveal how the working population in towns and countryside remain normally engaged in the production of goods and services for pay, profit of family gain.

Employment Patterns: This work or employment pattern in the rural areas is naturally different from that in the urban areas. The data presented in Table,

Table 46:

- ### Percentage of Unemployed to Persons in Labor Force for Population of Age 15-59 based on Weekly Activity Status.

SL. NO	STATES/UNION TERRITORY	PERCENTAGE OF UNEMPLOYED TO PERSONS IN LABOR FORCE OF POPULATION OF AGE 15-59			
		BASED ON WEEKLY ACTIVITY STATUS			
		RURAL		URBAN	
		Male	Female	Male	Female
1	Andhra Pradesh	3.86	6.85	7.56	16.34
2	Assam	1.66	0.90	5.01	16.99
3	Bihar	4.66	3.52	6.98	11.02
4	Gujarat	2.29	1.27	6.48	7.74
5	Haryana	5.75	0.46	6.83	6.94
6	Himachal Pradesh	1.20	0.00	5.50	4.97
7	Jammu & Kashmir	1.04	1.59	3.54	14.45

8	Karnataka	3.95	3.29	6.57	7.49
9	Kerala	11.09	11.36	13.62	12.20
10	Madhya Pradesh	0.91	0.54	3.48	4.55
11	Maharastra	2.86	2.58	8.19	20.92
12	Meghalaya	-	-	1.67	8.59
13	Nagaland	-	-	0.00	0.00
14	Orissa	4.03	3.82	7.32	14.67
15	Punjab	3.17	1.06	3.83	7.61
16	Rajasthan	0.86	0.76	5.28	0.70
17	Tamil Nadu	6.46	6.02	10.41	12.40
18	Uttar Pradesh	2.53	1.23	5.71	5.92
19	West Bengal	5.20	5.16	10.42	15.56
20	Chandigarh	-	-	0.00	20.17
21	Delhi	9.14	0.00	7.64	30.33
22	Gao, Daman & Diu	12.89	1.72	11.16	7.01
23	Pondicherry	8.00	8.68	15.38	0.00
	All India	9.68	8.68	15.38	0.00

• **Source: Governament Of India., National Sample Survey, 27ᵗʰ round, p. 68.**

will show that in rural India the self-employment sector is much largeas copared to the wage employment sector. It is observed that of the total rural population, persons working on own account in farm and non-form enterprises togarher with those working as helpers in household farm and non-farm enterprises constitutes 33.30 per cent, whereas persons engaed on regular wage and salary earners in farm or non- farm enterprises togather with the casual wage earners constitute only17.41 per cent. But, it should be noted that of the percentage total self-employed (33.36%), the percentage of persons working as helpers in household farm and non-farm enterprises is as large as 14.93. Helpers in household enterprises do not usually work intensively and they work intermittently also. The term by which they are categorized itself indicates that they are deployed in the household enterprises only at the time of pressing need and a sizeable proportion of them, particularly the females, are normally engaged in essential household work.

Also, in the rural areas of all the States the self employment sector is larger than the wage-employment sector. Only their relative proportions is different in different States. Where the deviation from the all India rural average is relatively latge has been illustrated below for each of the usual activity category separately. In Assam (17.56 percent), Himachal Pradesh (22.22 percent), Madhya Pradesh (16.69 percent), Meghalaya (45.83 percent), Rajasthan (20.13 percent), Uttar Pradesh (19.79 percent), Jammu & Kashmir (22.40 percent), Manipur (20.26 percent), the proportion of persons working in own farm of the respective rural population are more than the all India average which is 14.51 per cent of the total rural-population. The proportion of the total rural population of persons working in household non-farm enterprises in Andhra Pradesh (4.62 percent), Kerala (5.90 percent), Punjab (5.95 per cent), Tamil Nadu (5.84 per cent), Uttar Pradesh (4.67 percent), Delhi (10.29 percent), Gao (4.80 percent), Pondicherry (4.82 percent), Manipur (7.76 percent) and Tripura (4.63 percent) are above the all-India average of 3.86 percent.

The proportion of regular salaried employess/wages labourers in farm (the majority or whome are probably bonded agricultural labourers and regular farm servents) of the respective total rural populationare very low in Himachal Pradesh (0.74 percent), Kerala (1.12 percent), Rajastan (0.91 percent), Delhi (1.32 percent), Pondicherry (1.51 percent), Jammu & Kashmir (0.32 percent), and Manipur (0.38 percent) compared to the all- India average of 2.97 percent of the all-India rural population. In bihar, however, the corresponding figures are rather high (5.00 percent). The proportions of persons working as regular salaried employees/wage labourers in non-farm enter- prise/business etc., in Kerala (5.65 percent), West Bengal (3.93 percent), Delhi (10.76 percent), Goa (4.80 percent) and Pondicherry (5.18 percent), are above the corresponding all-India average of 2.17 percent of the respective total rural population.

The proportions of persons working as casual wage labourer of the respective total rural population are very high in Andhra Pradesh (23.27 percent), Tamil Nadu (21.82 percent), Goa (20.34 percent) and Pondicherry (25.81 percent); moderately high in Karnataka (18.17 percent) and Maharastra (19.00 percent) and very low in Assam (3.15 percent), Haryana (4.42 percent), Himachal Pradesh (1.02 percent). Meghalaya (5.67 percent), Punjab (7.05 percent), Rajasthhan (3.00 percent), Uttar Pradesh (5.92 percent), Delhi (3.41 percent), Jammu & Kashmir (0.67 percent) and Manipur (1.02 percent) as compared to the corresponding all India average of 12.37 percent of the all-India rural population. It should be noted that in rural areas, this category by and large, represent the agricultural and other rural labour.

The proportions of persons working in household farm as unpaid helpers of the respective total rural population are significantly high in Hariyana (20.07 percent), Himachal Pradesh (25.50 percent), Karnataka (18.88 percent), Madhya Pradesh (25.41 percent), and Rajasthan (34.44 percent) in comparison to the all– India average of 13.50 percent of the total rural population. It is needless to mention that the high proportions of helpers, particularly in household farm, is symtomatic of the higher incidence of unemployment or under-utilisation of labour force in household farm economy. In this context, the high labour force participation rate, for all practical purposes, turns out to be a misleading index of the country's economy.

In urban areas the wage-employment sector is more important than the self-employment sector in so far as its capacity to offer work or employment is concerned. Persons self-employed in own farm or in household non-farm enterprise togather constitute only 15.29 percent of the total allIndia urban population. In this sector the share of the unpaid helpers (farm qand non-farm combined) and of the persons working in own farm is 3.94 percent and 1.43 percent respectively of the total all-India urban population. It is clearly seen that in the urban self employment sector, the substantive contribution to the total gainful work comes from persons working in non-farm household enterprise, business, profession, etc., who constitutes only 9.92 percent of the total all-India urban population. In contrast to what has been observed in the self-employment sector, persons working as wage and salaried employee/ wage earners, in non-farm enterprise, businessprofessin, etc., occupies a dominent position in urban-areas. They constitute 17.32 percent of the total allIndia urban population. In this sector the other constituents are casual labourers and those who work as wage/salaried employes in farms. The respective proportion is 4.39 percent and 0.44 percent of the total All-India urban population.

Like the all-India urban work pattern, in the urban areas of all the States also the wage-employment sector has been found to be more important compared to the self employment sector though their relative proportions are different in different States. Only the intenceof larger deviation from the All-India urban situation are brought out below inrespect of each of the activity categories. In Kerala (2.71 percent), Nagaland (3.38 percent), Rajasthan (3.03 percent) and Manipur (4.62 percent), the proportion of persons working in household,own farm to the respective urban population

is higher than the All-India urban average of 1.43 percent. In Meghalaya (3.96 percent), Nagaland (1.88 percent), Chandigarh (1.79 percent), and Goa (5.18 percent), the proportion of persons working in household non-farm enterprise/profession is much low than the All-India urban average of 9.62 percent.

The All-India average of persons working as regular salaried employee/wage labourer is relatively very low (0.44 percent) as compared to the proportions of the other constitutents of the working population. But only in assam (1.26 percent) and Nagaland (5.26 percent),their proportion to the respective urban population is rather high. In Himachal Pradesh (24.49 percent), Maharastra (22.59 percent), Nagaland (30.63 percent), Delhi (24.48 percent) and Goa (21.62 percent), the proportion of persons working as wage/salaried employee in non-farm enterprise/profession to their respective urban population is relatively high as compared to the All-India urban average of 17.32 percent.

The proportion to the respective total urban population of persons working as casual labourers in Andhra Pradesh (6.35 percent),Gujarat (5.95 percent), Kerala (8.54 percent), Orissa (5.72 percent), Tamil Nudu (5.37 percent), and Goa (5.92 percent) is higher than the corresponding All-India average of 4.39 percent. Persons categorised as helpers in farm and non-farm households enterprise to the total All-India urban population is 0.98 percent and 2.96 percent. Only in Rajasthan, the proportion of households farm and household non-farm helpers (3.82 percent and 5.11 percent respectively) are much higher than the corresponding All-India urban averages.

CHAPTER VII

CHARACTERISTICS OF UNEMPLOYMENT

Three different measures of unemployment have been obtained from the 27th Round Survey. By a measure of unemployment, is ment only the measure of open or overt unemployment and the visible under-employment. Measurements of disguised or hidden unemployment was not attempted in this survey. On the basis of clasification of individual members of households by usual status, percentage estimates were obtained of the number of persons chronically unemployed for different States, seperately for rural and urban population respectively as base. In Table XI will show that in rural areas normally very few people report as usually not having any gainful work and openly seeking or avilable for employment.

Table 47

- **Percentage of Unemployed to Persons in Labour Force for Population of age 15-59 on the Basis of Weakly Activity Status**

SL.NO.	STATES	RURAL		URBAN	
		MALE	FEMALE	MALE	FEMALE
1	Andhra Pradesh	3.86	6.85	7.55	16.34
2	Assam	1.66	0.90	5.01	16.00

3	Bihar	4.66	3.52	6.98	11.02
4	Gujarat	2.29	1.27	6.48	7.74
5	Haryana	5.75	0.46	6.83	6.94
6	Himachal Pradesh	1.20	0.00	5.50	4.07
7	Jammu & Kashmir	1.04	1.59	3.54	14.45
8	Karnataka	3.95	3.20	6.57	7.49
9	Kerala	11.09	11.36	13.62	12.20
10	Madhya Pradesh	0.97	0.54	3.48	4.55
11	Maharastra	2.86	2.58	8.10	20.92
12	Meghalaya	-	-	1.67	8.59
13	Nagaland	-	-	0.00	0.00
14	Orissa	4.03	3.82	7.32	14.67
15	Punjab	3.17	1.06	3.83	7.61
16	Rajasthan	0.86	0.76	5.28	0.70
17	Tamil Nadu	6.46	6.02	10.41	12.40
18	Uttar Pradesh	2.53	1.23	5.71	5.92
19	West Bengal	5.20	5.16	10.42	16.56
20	Chandighar	-	-	0.00	20.17
21	Delhi	9.14	0.00	7.64	30.33
22	Goa, Daman & Diu	12.89	1.72	11.16	7.01
23	Pondichery	8.00	8.68	15.38	0.00
	All India	3.68	8.68	15.38	0.00

• **Source: op. Cit., p.68.**

Never the figures for unemployed persons thrown-up from the survey data for different States are not so small as can be dismissed as insignificant. Moreover, for the States of West Bengal and Bihar, the estimates are nearly 1 percent and for Kerala (2.42 percent), Goa (1.57 percent) and Pondicherry (2.01 percent), the percentages are rather on the higher side. In case of Karnataka (0.38 percent) which is less than 1 percent. In view of the rural population base being massive, the estimates in terms of actual number of unemployed persons will be quite large to cause concern. The situation in urban areas, however, is far worse, excepting, in the State of Meghalaya, Uttar Pradesh, Rajasthan and Jammu & Kashmir. In case of Karnataka (1.93 percent) as against to the All-India (2.05 percent) figure.

A more precise and meaningful form the point of view of policy purpose indicators of the measure of chronic unemployment can be obtained by expressing the number of usual unemployed persons as percentage of persons in labour-force (which largely excludes children and old). In Karnataka the rate of incidence of unemployment in rural areas (0.65 percent) as against to (1.01 percent) of All-India. In urban areas (4.91 percent) as against (5.18 percent) of All-India figure. The immensity of the problem can be properly realised if the rates for both male and female population in the labour force in rural as well as urban areas are examined from Table XI.

It is evident from Table 4 that the rate of unemployment is very high in rural areas of Andhra Pradesh (9.61 percent), Bihar (10.17 percent), Kerala (24.26 percent), Orissa (9.32 percent), Tamil Nadu (10.63 percent), West Bengal (9.55 percent), Goa (25.12 percent), Karnataka (9.04 percent), Pondicherry (19.19 percent), and Jammu & Kashmir (14.36 percent). In the rural areas of Gujarat (6.08 percent), Maharastra (8.64 percent), Rajasthan (4.41 percent) and Manipur (7.33 percent), the rate is moderately high. In the urban areas, however,the rate is very high in Andhra Pradesh (12.47 percent), Bihar (8.48 percent), Haryana (8.16 percent), Kerala (23.33 percent), Maharastra (8.43 percent), Goa (8.88 percent), Pondicherry (12.73 percent) and Tripura (11.82 percent) and moderately high in Gujarat (6.34 percent), Karnataka (7.64 percent), Orissa (7.15 percent), Punjab (6.46 percent), Jammu & Kashmir (6.56 percent) and Manipur (6.45 percent).

· Change In The Structure Of Employment

In a study like this we face the almost interactable problem of non-comparability of the Indan census data on working force, which is the consequeuece of ever changing concept and difinations. Considering the present employment–unemployment scenario in the country, the Elevent Five Year Plan strategizes rapid growth in employment opportunities along with improvement in the quality of employment. It recognizes the need to increase the share of regular employment in total employment and a correspondig reduction in casual employment. Attempts to introduce conceptual refinements regarding the definition of 'worker' from census to census. The 1971 census data on working force are all the more non-comparable with those of the earlier censuses because, for the first time in the history of Indian Census it introduced the concept of 'main activity',[12] to cover full-time workers only. The instruction to enumerators clearly laid down that persons engaged in household duties or a studies, who participated in the family economic activity on a less than full time basis, should not be classified as having work as their 'main activity', whereas most of these persons would have been included in the working force under the difination of 1961 census. As a result, the participation rate of workers fell from 42.08 in 1961 to 33.54 in 1971 (the lowest ever recorded in Indian Census) by22% the decrese in the participation rates of females being more steep, 52.86%, from 27.96% in 1961 to13.18 in 1971. Of cource, the marginal workers were sought to be netted in the category of 'secondary work' in 1971.While the statewise data on secondary workers engaged in secondary from five percent sample data for the All-India shows that avery small proportion of the non-workers reported some economic activity in 1981. The gap between the work participation rates of males in 1961 and 1971 tends to close in most States if the 1961 data are so adjusted that workers aged 15 and over in the rural areas, and those in the age group 15-54 in the urban areas, are considered economically active. It is not possible to establish any workable comparability for female workers.

· Inter-Sectaral Changes in Working Force 1961-1971.

We may now study the changes in sectoral distribution of working force during the decade 19611971. Table 4.1 below shows that Kerala, West Bengal, Tamil Nadu, Maharastra,Gujarat, Punjab and Andhra Pradesh had above India proportion of working force engaged in the non-primary sectors taken togather in 1961. These States

---

[12] 12For criticisma of this criterian see the following:

(a) J.N.Sinha; "A Rational View of Census Economic Data"

(b) Srinivasan, K.N., and Sharma. R.N., "on making comparisons of the data of Economically Active Population col-lected in the census of India, 1961 and 1971;

(c)Kalra. B.R., "A Preliminary aprisal of 1971 Census Economic Results', paper submitted to the Seminar on First Results of the 1971 Census Of India, Nov., 1971.

generally had above India proportions separately in the secondary and tertiary sector as well, except that Karnataka too had above India proportion in the secondary sector, while Andhra Pradesh had below India proportion in the tertiary sector. The only changes since then had been that Karnataka came to have above India proportion in the nonprimary sectors taken together. The coefficients of rank correlation between the two rank orders of States in 1961 and 1971 are 0.91 and 0.95 in the primary, secondary and tertiary sector respectively.

Table 48

· Sectoral Distribution of Male Working Forces

1971					
STATES	PRIMARY SECTOR	SECONDARY	SECTOR NON-HOUSEHOLD INDUSTRY	TERTIARY	SECTOR OTHER SERVICES
Andhra Pradesh	69.93	11.94	4.97	18.13	8.54
Assam	76.67	4.89	1.13	18.44	9.65
Bihar	83.45	5.89	2.88	10.57	5.21
Gujarat	65.12	14.85	10.42	20.03	8.78
Jammu & Kashmir	71.13	9.08	3.84	10.79	11.65
Kerala	54.97	6.46	11.19	28.57	12.53
Madhya Pradesh	78.79	8.32	3.75	12.80	7.17
Maharastra	59.90	17.44	12.53	22.67	10.21
Karnataka	69.83	12.16	6.46	18.01	8.26
Orissa	80.84	6.01	2.33	13.15	8.27
Punjab	65.55	12.44	4.32	22.01	12.11
Rajasthan	75.60	8.33	3.50	16.08	8.83

Tamilnadu	61.58	15.92	9.99	22.50	9.53
Uttra Pradesh	76.95	8.22	3.91	14.83	8.50
West Bengal	61.76	15.49	11.89	22.75	9.95
All India	70.38	11.32	6.61	18.30	9.08

- **Source: (1) Census Of India, Paper 3 of 1972; *Economic Characteris of Population.***

During the decade 1961-71, the proportion of male workers increased in the primary sector, and declined in the secondary and tertiary sectors in the country as a whole and in all the States separately, the only exceptions being Jammu & Kashmir and Maharastra in each sector, Assam, Kerala and Tamil Nadu in the secondary sector seperately and Karnataka in the tertiory sector above. It may be noted that changes in the proportions in the exception States were very low, except in Jammu & Kashmir. In this connection, we may note two other changes. First, the proportions of male workers employed in the secondary sector declined, or increased slightly, in most of the States, despite on increase in proportions in the non-household industry. Second, the tertiary sector proportions generally declined primarily because of the decline in proportions in other services segment in the tertiary sector, which tends to absorb all the sundry. The implication of these changes is that increase in the proportions of the primary sector in most of the States has been caused, mainly by decline in the proportions of workers engaged in the household industry and 'other services'. And this may have meant substitution of one-type of unemployment for another.

We now proceed to get further insight from the sectoral distribution of the addition to working force, total and rural, during 1961-1971. Table 5., shows that during the decade!961-71 81.3% of the total increase in male working force (2.97 crores) in the country as a whole was absorbed in the primary sector as against 6.6%, in the secondary, and 12.1% in the tertiary sector.

Table 49

- Number of people employed per 1000 people (WFPR0 according to usual status during 1972-73 to 2009-2010

ROUND (YEAR)	CATEGORY OF WORKERS	USUALLY EMPLOYED								
		RURAL			URBAN			ALL		
		Male	Felame	Total	Male	Female	Total	Male	Female	Total
66th (2009-10)	PS	537	202	374	539	119	339	538	180	365
	SS Only	10	59	34	4	19	11	8	48	27
	All	547	261	408	543	138	350	546	228	392
61th (2004-05)	PS	535	242	391	541	135	346	536	215	380
	SS Only	11	85	48	8	31	19	11	72	40
	All	546	327	439	549	166	365	547	267	420
55th (1999-2000)	All	531	299	417	518	139	337	527	259	397
50th (1993-1994)	All	553	328	444	521	155	347	545	286	420
43rd (1987-1988)	All	539	323	434	596	152	337	531	285	412

38th (1983)	All	547	340	445	512	151	340	538	296	420
32nd (1978)	All	552	331	444	508	156	341	543	297	423
27th (1973)	All	545	318	*	501	134	*	*	*	*

• *Ps = principle status, ss= secondary status*. proportions not derived for 27th round*

In table 45 the worker-population ratios (WPR's) for two categories of usual status workers viz., (a)usual principal status workers i.e., workers according to usual status (ps) and (b) usual subsidiary status workers i.e., persons working only in a subsidiary status (ss workers). In table above, the WPR's are presented for the years 1977-78, 1983, 1987-88, 1993-94, 1999-2000, and 2009-10 separately for usual status, secondary status. The two categories together constitute the total usually employed (or all workers) i.e., workers according to the usual status (ps+ss). The first category pertains to those with more or less stable employment. Work Participation Rate figures corresponding to 'all workers' in table 5.1 shows that 55 percent of the male and 23 percent of the females were workers.

Bihar, Orissa, Uttar Pradesh, Kerala, Madhya Pradesh and West Bengal recorded above India absorption of additional working force in primary sector, while Rajasthan and Andhra Pradesh were only slightly short of the National Rate of absorption. It may be noted that all these States except Madhya Pradesh and Rajasthan recorded decline in employment in 'other services' while only Kerala and west Bengal recorded above India rates of absorption in the secondary sector as well. Bihar and Uttar Pradesh recorded a decline in the working force in the secondary sector during the decade, the former even in the tertiary sector. However, even these States recorded an increase in the non-household manufacuring employment. In Jammu & Kashmir, Maharastra, Karnataka, Tamil Nadu, Gujarat and Punjab the share of the primary sector in the additional working force was below, and that of secondary and tertiary sectors seperately above, the national average. All States except Assam and jammu & Kashmir suffered a decline in employment in household industry, and many States in 'Other Services' too.

As for the addition to rural working force,increase in the male rural working force engaged in the primary sector exceeded the total increase in the rural working force by 3.3% in the country as a whole, the excess being much larger in U P., Bihar, Tamil Nadu, Orissa, Kerala and West Bengal and almost equal to the All India average in Gujarat and Madhya Pradesh. In other States,except Assam and Jammu & Kashmir, more than 90% of the additional rural working force was absorbed in the primary sector. While it is possible to have ecnmic development without population transfers from the agriculture to the non-agricultural sector.[13] The possible reverse shift from the more productive urban areas to the less productive rural areas is indicative of acute unemployment situation in the urban areas, which force the marginal rural migrants to go back to the village to share work with their family. Since their already existed considerable volume of unemployment and under-employment in the rural areas the situation would have deteriorated further during the decade.

There is ample evidence to suggest that this has been so,through no firm estimates of rural unemployment are available. The incidence of unemployment in rural India (all ages males) reached the all time high figure of 11.82. The Planning Commission estimated that rural unemployment increased from about 5.8 million in 1960-61 to about 7 million in 1965-66. The estimated rural unemploment incresed from about 5.8 million to about 7 million. The earlier practice of giving estimates of unemployment has been abandoned by the Planning Commission on the recommendations of the committee of experts on unemployment estimates, which was of the view " that estimates of growth in the labour force, of additional employment generated by the plans and of unemployment at the end of the plan periods presented in one dimensional magnitudes are neither menigful nor useful as indicators of the economic situation"[14] However, this view of the committee has not gone unchallenged. Making use of the NSS data on household consumption, the estimation of poverty of at least 30% of the rural population. Making use of NSS data, the estimation of the number of the wholly unemployed and severely unemployed available for work is about 2.15 million, 1.93 million in the rural areas and 22 lakhs in the urban areas.

The preceeding analysis shows that despite an increase of 41% in the netnational product and of 13.3% in the per capita income (at 1960-61 prices) during the period 1960-61 to 1970-71 as a result of the public sector expenditure of about Rs. 20,000 crores during the decade, the presure of population on agriculture and allied industries has increased. Thus, changes in the industrial distribution of working force seem to run counter to the Clark fisher hypothesis that "..... as time goes on and communities become more economically advanced, the numbers engaged in agricultural tend to decline relative to the numbers engaged in services"[15] They further show that the planners took a very optimistic view of the prospect of growth of national income and population. It was thought on the eve of second plan that the projected relative decline of the proportion

---

[13] Khusro.A.m., Economic Development with No Population Transfers, Institute of Economic Growth, Occasional pa-per No. 4.

[14] Planning Commision : Reports of the Committee of Experts on Unemployment Estimates. p.31.

[15] Clark. Colin: Conditions of Economic Progress.

employed in agriculture by about 13% while the national income goes up by 100% would be in keeping with the historical experience in other countries..

We estimate the incidence of rural poverty across all three social groups, and relates this to their demographic, educational and occupational characterstics. An important issue that we need to address in determining the poverty status of households is the choice of the poverty line.

Table. 50

- ## Sectoral Distribution of increase in Male Working Force 196—71

STATES	PRIMARY SECTOR	SECONDARY SECTOR HOUSEHOLD INDUSTRY	NON HOUSEHOLD INDUSTRY	CONCENTRATED	TOTAL
Andhra Pradesh	80.2	-9.3	10.1	2.9	3.7
Assam	77.4	2.5	2.9	0.5	5.9
Bihar	106.5	-4.3	2.2	-0.1	-2.2
Gujarat	74.2	-5.7	14.2	1.9	10.4
Jammu & Kashmir	53.2	4.9	3.4	8.1	16.4
Kerala	90.7	-3.3	16.5	4.0	17.2
Madhya Pradesh	87.4	-2.9	6.0	-1.2	1.9
Maharastra	56.5	-3.1	19.8	2.0	18.7
Karnataka	71.3	-3.0	10.8	0.7	8.5
Orissa	97.3	-4.4	6.0	0.6	2.2
Punjab	79.3	-7.4	9.0	1.5	3.1
Rajasthan	81.1	-3.8	6.7	0.2	3.1

Tamil Nadu	71.4	-5.5	20.4	1.7	16.6
Uttar Pradesh	96.9	-7.5	6.7	-1.0	-1.8
West Bengal	84.3	0.8	8.3	-1.0	7.9
All India	81.3	-4.5	10.1	0.9	6.6

As attempt is made here to examine the nature of the empirical data being made available during the last three decades through condinuous large scale sample surveys into the employment and level of living of people in rural and urban areas. Attention will be confined to only two problems, namely the extent of change in employment and level of living (or expenditure) as well as of income of the rural labourers or the weaker section in rural areas, the two being largely co-terminus. It is not necessary to try to justify the selection of these two aspects which at present occupy uppermost positions in our thinking on planning and policy making. With the data from the 25th round of the National Sample Survey, devoted specially to the weaker sections, now gradually becoming available, these questions are again going to be discussed threadbare.

Table.51

- **Sectoral Distribution of Increase in Male Working force 1971**

STATES	TERTIARY SECTOR				INCREASE IN RURAL WORKERS
	TRADE AND COMMERCE	TRANSPORT	OTHER SERVICES	TOTAL	
Andhra pradesh	10.9	5.6	-0.4	16.1	98.5
Assam	9.4	4.4	3.0	16.8	55.2
Bihar	4.4	1.1	-9.3	-4.2	115.2
Gujarat	11.2	4.5	-0.03	15.4	103.0
Jammu & Kashmir	10.9	11.9	7.6	30.4	64.7

Kerala	26.4	9.1	-43.4	-7.9	107.2
Madhya Pradesh	5.5	2.1	3.1	10.7	102.8
Maharastra	15.4	4.3	5.1	24.8	90.0
Karanataka	13.5	8.2	-1.5	20.2	82.0
Orissa	8.1	3.8	11.4	0.5	108.5
Punjab	8.7	2.5	6.3	17.5	92.1
Rajastan	6.0	2.8	6.9	15.7	97.2
Tamil Nadu	19.7	8.9	-16.8	12.0	111.0
Uttar Pradesh	4.6	2.3	-2.0	4.9	118.8
West Bengal	8.6	6.7	-7.5	7.8	104.9
All India	10.3	4.6	-2.8	12.1	103.3

• Has Rural Unemployment Declined?

This Chapter is divided into two parts; in the first part the estimates of employment of rural labour or weaker sections will be examined and in the second data on consumption or levels of living as well as the income of this class will be considered. Despite all the limitations frequently pointed out and noted the data on employment in the rural sector made available by the National Sample Survey from time to time are being used to estimate the extent of labour time of the labour force spent in gainful employment and unemployment. In view of the repeated survey of this aspect by the N.S.S., comparison of the estimates of employment and unemployment over time is inevitable. Broadly speaking, two distinct sets of surveys into rural employment have been undertaken and reported by the N.S.S. organization. One set relates to estimates of emnployment unemployment of the entire rural population. The other relates to only some well defined section of the rural population. In 1956-57 the N.S.S. organization conducted a sample survey into the various aspects including employment-of agricultural labourers, for the second enquiry into agricultural labourers in India. In 1963-64 a similar enquiry was also conducted for the third survey of rural labour in India. While naturally the universes of these three surveys were not identical, they were largely the same, as we shall see below.

We propose to examine the changing positions of employment-unemployment of the "Weaker sections" or the agricultural labourers, based on the Second Agricultural Labour Enquiry and the 25th round of the N.S.S. The employment data for the entire rural population collected during the other N.S.S. rounds will be used for comparison.

For the 25th round of the N.S.S. in 1970-71 the 'weaker section' of the rural sector, was defined to consist of: (a) the non-cultivating labour households, and (b) the lowest 10% of the households cultivating some land. On the basis of these data it is possible to examine the extent of employment and unemployment of the 'weaker section' in our rural society.

The 'weaker section' of the rural society, as defined above, is largely, if not entirely, conterminous with agricultural labour households as defined in the second agricultural labourer enquiry in 1956-57. One part of the "weaker section" consists of all rural households without any land to cultivate personally and deriving their income mainly from wage earnings. The second agricultural labour enquiry also covered the same population (agricultural labourers households without land) except that it excluded all such wage-earning households who derived the bulk of their earnings from non-agricultural labour. But this is a small proportion of all labour households, and cannot be considered to have very different conditions of employment.[1]

Another part of the 'weaker section' consists of the lowest 10% of the cultivators. The second ALE, on the other hand, considered only such cultivating households as agricultural labourer households as earned the larger part of their income from agricultural labour. Defined this way the agricultural labour households with land may constitute more or less than 10% of all cultivating households depending upon the specific situation. It would, therefore, useful to compare, the two population covered by these two surveys.

In Table 51, the% of the two subclasses of the 'weaker section' and their total to the total agricultural households in each State in 1970-71. Similarly columns (5), (6) and (7) of the same Table give the% of agricultural labour households with land, without land and their total, to the total number of rural households in 1956-57. In appears that while the weaker section in 1970-71 constituted about 28% of the agricultural househelds, the agricultural labour household in 195657 constituted over 24% of all rural household. If the weaker section household in 1970-71 could be

1. The Third Rural Labor Enquiry shows that in 1963-64 while rural labour households formed 17.2% of all rural households, agricultural labour households formed 14.2%. The difference of 3% is accounted for by the non-agricultural labour households.

2. The 'agricultural households' excludes all rural households deriving more or less regular and major income from self-employment in trading establishments, manufacturers, mechanized transport, professions, or from rent or salaried employment. The estimate of such rural households is not available and expressed, like in the second A.L.E. as a% of all rural households it would be nearer the A.L.E. proportion.

It is more interesting to note that the landless labour households in 1970-71 constituted over 20% of all agricultural households, while the landless agricultural labour households in 195657 constituted about 14% of all rural households. A part of the difference between these two estimates may be explained by the facts that (a) the landless labour households in 1970-71 are being expressed as a percentage of total agricultural households and not of the larger total rural households, and (b) the A.L.E. data excludes non-agricultural labour households. But a larger part of the difference is likelyu to be real; i.e., it reflects an increase in the proportion of labndless laboring households in rural India since 1956-57. This is corroborated by the comparison of the census figures for 1961 and 1971, which shows that the population of agricultural labourers in India had recorded an increase of 80% over the decade, whereas that of cultivators increased by only about 4%. While the agricultural labourers in the census include both these with land as well as those without land, yet it would be proper to infer-from the above that the proportion of landless labourers in the rural population had recorded distinct increase between 1956-57 and 1970-71.

Table 52

Percentage of Weaker Section Households With and Without Land Cultivated Holdings to Total Rural Agricultural Households in the 25th Round N.S.S. and the Percentage of Agricultural Laborer Rural Household in 1956-57.

	STATES	NSS 25th Round (1970-71) Percentage of agricultural households constituting weaker sections			2nd A.L.E. (1956-57) Percentage of rural households classed as agricultural labour households	
		With land	Without Land	Total	With Land	Without Land
1	Uttar Pradesh	8.81	11.91	20.72	9.58	7.66
2	Madhya Pradesh	8.53	14.74	23.27	9.94	14.59
3	Bihar	8.23	17.72	25.95	18.09	11.46
4	West Bengal	NA	NA	NA	9.13	15.87
5	Orissa	8.16	18.41	26.57	14.67	15.74
6	Assam	9.24	7.55	16.79	6.72	11.46
7	Andhra Pradesh	6.52	34.78	41.30	12.19	23.40
8	Tamil Nadu	5.98	40.16	46.14	13.62	22.92
9	Kerala	9.39	6.10	15.49	11.73	11.00
10	Maharashtra	7.62	23.80	31.42	8.67	17.36
11	Gujarat	8.11	18.90	27.01		
12	Mysore	7.88	21.15	29.03	9.87	17.40
13	Rajasthan	9.27	7.28	16.55	1.57	4.33

14	Punjab	8.87	11.28	20.15	0.87	8.51
15	Haryana	6.90	30.95	37.85		
	ALL INDIA	7.96	20.37	28.33	10.49	13.98

- **Source: G.O.I., National Sample Survey, 25th Round, 1970-71.**

Unlike the class of landless labourers, the proportion of labourer households with some cultivated land was not very different: 8% in 1970-71 and 10.5% in 1956-57. Here the difference is largely due to the arbitrary figure—the smallest of 10% of the weaker section, while the second A.L.E. had an income criterion for selection. Consequently, one finds the agricultural labourers in Punjab, Haryana and Rajasthan in 1956-57 forming a much smaller proportion of rural households than in 1970-71 while those in States like Bihar, Orissa, Andhra Pradesh and Tamil Nadu much more. Besides this arbitratiness, it is possible, on the grounds stated in para 9 above, to presume that the class of agricultural labourers in 1970-71 defined as in the 2nd A.L.E. would, form a larger percentage of the cultivating households in 1970-71 than in 1956-57. All in all, it is not improper to conclude from this that the coverages of the two surveys, the 2nd A.L.E. and the 25th round 'weaker section', are largely comparable.

The 25th round of N.S.S. gives data on total time spent by persons in the small cultivators and landless labour households in gainful employment, in seeking job and in not being available for gainful employment, classified by age and sex. We shall confine ourselves to the adult males between ages 15 and 59 only. The children, that is those below 15 years, are by and large outside the labour market. The same cannot be said about all persons aged 60 or above; but for meaningful assessment and comparison, we shall exclude them also. Female employment and particularly unemployment, are more difficult to assess and so we shall keep it aside for our purpose.

Table 15 summarises the total time disposition of the adult males in the 'weaker section' households. It shows that the adult males spent 82% of their normal working hours during the year 1970-71 in gainful employment (on own business or wage labour). Only 5.7% of their total time was spent in unemployment, i.e., in seeking work or being available for work. The remaining 12.5% of the time they were not available for work due to sickness, domestic work, festivities, etc. Onlyu in 5 of the 14 States for which data are available, was the percentage of time spent in unemployment larger than 5.7; Andhra Pradesh, Bihar, Kerala, Punjab and Tamil nadu. The average percentage of time spent in unemployment was even smaller—3.4%–among the small cultivators, and only a little larger—6.5%– among the landless labourers. For most of the States the averages were less than these all-India averages. Indeed, for some States like Orissa, Madhya Pradesh and Mysore, and

Assam and U.P. as well, the time spent by the adult male workers in unemployment was quite small; less than 1 or 2 per cent.

The above findings of the 25th round of the N.S.S. run counter to the general impressions or presumptions about the extent of available employment and prevailing unemployment in the rural areas of the country in general and in some of the States in particular which are among the poorest in India. Indeed, while 4 or 5% unemployment may be quite high by standard of the developed countries, it may not acquire the same significance in rural India if it is remembered that this measures not chronically unemployed persons, but total time spent in unemployment by all the adult males in the 'weaker section' population. The estimate of unemployment time based on the 25th round of the N.S.S. appears even more disturbing when it is compared with the estimate of time spent in unemployment by the adult male casual agricultural labourers in 1956-57 as shown by the second A.L.E. These data are also presented in Table side-by-side those for the 25th round of the N.S.S.

It appears from Table that in 1956-57 the adult male casual agricultural labourers in India were engaged in gainful employment for only 65% of the time, and were unemployment for 18.6% of the time. For 16.4% of the time they were not available for gainful work. This is in sharp contrast to the 82% time spent in gainful employment and only 5.7% of the time in unemployment by the adult males in the 'weakers section' (a very comparable group) in 1970-71. Is one to infer from this that there has been a significant increase in the employment available to 'weaker section' of the rural labourers in the 14 years since 1956-57 and a consequent decline in unemployment in their ranks, so much so that rural unemployment had lost it urgency by 1970-71? Before-one comes to any such startling conclusion by a simple comparison of the data from the two surveys, it is prudent to go behind them and look for any differences in concepts and methods that may be responsible for such wide divergence between the two estimates.

Examination of the methods and concepts used in the two surveys reveals a relevant difference in the approach used to measure intensities of time disposition. In the 25th round of N.S.S. the time disposition of each member of the sample household on each of the 7 days preceding the day of enquiry was to be noted. But this was to be noted not in hours but in days. For nothing the intensity of occupation in various activities an intensity of occupation in various activities an intensity code was specified. If the intensity of time dispotion on any day was ½ or more, i.e., if a person had spent more than half of this normal working day on any particular activity, then the intensity was to be recorded as 1. If the intensity was ½ or leass it was to be noted as ½.[3] As against this, the second A.L.E. laid down that a full days work (intensity 1) will mean ¾ or more of normal working hours. More than ¼ and less than ¾ of the normal hours was taken to constitute work with half intensity. And less than ¼ work has considered as 'normal intensity' which was to be equal to 1/8 of a normal working day. Work done for less tha this intensity (i.e., 1/8 day) was to be ignored. The normal working day was taken to be of 10 hours duration.

The difference between the 2nd A.L.E. and the 25th round of N.S.S. in regard to noting the intensity of time disposition might partly at least account for the difference in the findings of the two surveys in their estimation of employment and unemployment. Unfortunately, however, the available tabulated data relating to them do not leave any scope for adjusting one set to conform more or less to the definitions of the other, so that extent of divergence due to this difference in measurements may be broadly indicated.

We may, however, try to get over this difficulty by uising the employment data for all rural males from the other N.S.S. rounds. These data are available in a form that permits some maneuverability in regard to the measurement of intensity. Attention may, therefore, be turned to these data.The N.S.S. in the 14th, 15th, 17th and 19th rounds (from 1958 to 1964-65) collected data on employment of the rural population. The tabulated results are made available only for the country as a whole. They show the sex-wise division of the rural population into those that were in the labour force and those that were outside it, during the week labour force and those that were outside it, during the week under reference. The information about the detailed activity pattern of the working population during the reference week is presented in two ways. One set of Tables gives the division of the 7 days among various activities like employment, unemployment or not available for work. But since the intensity of each activity is not measured in either the way the A.L.E. or the 25th round set out to measure it, these Tables are not very useful for our purpose. The second set of Tables gives a classification of persons in the rural labour force according to the total number of hours spent by them during the reference week in gainful employment. These data appear, subject to certain limitations, adjustable for comparison with the [3. "The decision whether the intensity is ½ or 1 will depend on the judgement of the informant. In case of doubt and difficulty, however, attachment for 4 hours or less may be taken to ½ intensity and more than 4 hours attachment as intensity 1."]employment data given by the 2nd A.L.E. on the one hand and the 25th round of the N.S.S. on the other. We shall set this out in what follows.

Though data on the above lines are available from 4 different N.S.S. rounds for the purpose in hand, it is not necessary to examine them separately, but to take an average of all the four rounds.

The differences in the findings of these 4 rounds are not such as to make averaging unhelpful. For purposes of comparison attention shall be contained only to the employment of rural males.The N.S.S. tabulations show (a) the proportion of the total male population in the labour force, (b) the proportion of those in the labour force fully "unemployed" during the week under reference, (c) the proportion of those workers who were gainfully employed for 14 hours or less during the week, (d) the proportion of those employed for more than 14 to 28 hours in the week, (e) the proportion of workers gainfully employed for more than 28 to 42 hours in the week, and (f) the proportion of workers gainfully employed for more than 42 hours in the week.

Now, it is obvious that the male in the labour force according to these N.S.S. rounds are not necessarily the adult males of the 2nd A.L.E. or the males between 15-59 years of age of the 25th round for whom employment data were presented earlier in this study. The 'males in the labour force' might include some non-adults who were gainfully employed for at least one day during the reference week, while it might exclude adult males who were not gainfully employed or were seeking or available for work any time during the week. However, we do not expect this discrepancy between these male populations to create serious differences in estimation of employment in the 3 sets of surveys examined here. The relevant data relating to the rural males from the 4 N.S.S. rounds are summarized in Table 53 below.

Table 53

· **Pattern of Employment of the Rural Male Labour Force in India (Average of 4 N.S.S. rounds, 14th, 15th, 17th and 19th From 1958 to 1964-65)**

A	Proportions of rural males in the labour force		54.87%
B	Out of the total rural males in the labour force (A = 100%), the proportion	(i) Unemployed during the week	3.28%
		(ii) Employed for 14 hours or less in the week	5.60%
		(iii) Employed for 15 to 28 hours in the week	7.93%
		(iv) Employed for 29 to 42 hours in the week	15.76%
		(v) Employed for more than 42 hours in the week	65.43

With the help of the above Table, it is possible the estimate the total time spent by the male labour force in gainful employment, by using the alternative measures of intensity of time disposition adopted in the 25th round of the N.S.S. and the 2nd A.L.E. Let us first use the intensity measure of the 25th round of N.S.S. according to its engagement for more than half of a normal working day in any activity will be noted as intensity, that is a full work day and half-a-day or less will be noted as ½ intensity. Now, if a normal working day is considered as of 8 hours duration then a work week is equal to 56 hours duration. Persons gainfully employed for more than 28 hours may be treated as being fully employed during the week. All those unemployed for 28 hours or less may be considered as employed for only half the week. The rest of the time they as well as those reported as unemployed were either unemployed or were not available for work. Now the N.S.S. rounds do not give estimate of hours for which the workers were not available for work. But we may assume that on an average a rural male worker was not available for work 1/6th of the time (i.e., he was available for work for just over 300 days in a year). This is somewhat higher than the 12.5% time for which the adult male worker (15-59 years of age) were not available for work according to the 25th round. We, however, wish to have a higher estimate since some non-adults are also included in the 4th N.S.S. rounds considered here. Therefore, it can be calculated with the help of the above Table that the rural male labour force was 'unemployed' for about 7% of the time, following broadly the pattern of estimation followed in the 25th round. The estimate thus arrived at is not very different from the 5.7% unemployed time for the adult males among the 'weaker section' in the 25th round.

CHAPTER IX

SUMMARY AND CONCLUSIONS:

The 27th round (1972 October-September 1973) of the National Sample Survey was devoted to a survey of employment—unemployment in India. The 32nd found (July-September 1977) of the national Sample Survey was devoted to a survey of employment—unemployment in India.The estimates of employment, unemployment in this study dover all persons of 5 years of age and above. According to 1971 census, about 16% of the total population in Karnataka is below the age of 5 years.

The number of persons of 5 years and above in the State is estimated to 260.28 lakhs in 1973. Out of this population 120.00 lakhs are considered to be not in labour force and, therefore, they are reported to be not engaged in any gainful work and they also do not offer for work. The remaining population, that is 140.28 lakhs, constitute the labor force. Persons in the labor force are classified broadly into two subgroups:

1. those who are reported to work more or less fully or as helpers in own farm and non-farm business or as regular salaried or wage-earners; and

2. those who do not have a stable and adequate employment. The persons who are in first subgroup may be categorized as:

   - Working as full workers in own   37.54 lakhs
     farm or non-farm business
   - Working as helpers in farm and   42.44 lakhs
     non-farm helpers
   - Working as regular salaried or   19.27 lakhs
     wages workers

It can be stated that persons in categories (a) and (b) have a stable employment and their number is 56.81 lakhs. The work content of those who work as helpers in own farm and non-farm business (category 'b') is not known and such persons constitutes 42.44 lakhs. It is possible that a considerable number among them may not be having work throughout the period. These three categories together constitutes 99.25 lakhs or about 70% of the labour force.

The remaining 30% of the labour force, that is 41.03 lakhs do not have stable and adequate employment. This sub-group may be categorized as follows:

a) Working in own farm or non-farm business and also as casual wage workers 7.26 lakhs

b) Working as casual wage workers more or less adequately employed 10.64 lakhs

c) Working as casual workers intermittently unemployed and seeking work 21.14 lakhs

d) Persons with no work but seeking work or available for work 1.98 lakhs

It is the persons in the last two categories which should concern us most. The 1.98 lakhs persons who had not work and who were seeking work or were available for work may be termed as "chronically" unemployed. In order to meet their problem, it is necessary create about 2 lakhs additional full time jobs. In the case of 21.15 lakhs persons who are intermittently unemployed, they have to be provided with supplementary employment. Out of 21.15 lakhs casual wage workers who are intermittently unemployed, 19.82 lakhs are in rural areas and only 1.33 lakhs are in urban areas. It is generally known that the unemployed in the rural areas move into urban areas.

A large number of persons, particularly the casual wage earners in the rural areas, are unemployed and seek work intermittently throughout the year. Therefore, another measure of unemployment under-employment has also been derived. In addition to collection of information on usual activity of a person, information on his activity during the previous week has also been collected. A number of people reported that throughout the week they were seeking work or were available for employment but could not get any work. Their distribution in the rural and urban areas and by sex is as follows:

In interpreting these figures, we may bear in mind the following points: (a) the estimate of 5.78 lakhs persons unemployed and seeking work represents the average weekly situation during the period from October to March and the employment situation is likely to be worse during the months from April to September; (b) the estimate does not mean that 5.78 lakhs persons are unemployed throughout the year. It has been already stated that about 1.98 lakh persons are reported to be chronically unemployed. It is presumed that they will report themselves as unemployed every week of the year.

In addition to these 1.98 lakhs persons who are unemployed all the weeks of the years; a varying number is reported as unemployed each week. On an average, these number is 3.80 lakhs each week. Some of them may be unemployed just for one week of the year; others may be unemployed for more than one week of the year; but all of them are unemployed for at least one week at a stretch. But the estimate does mean that, on an average, each week about 5.78 lakh persons are reportedly unemployed throughout the week, are seeking work or are available for work but are unable to get work. Out of 5.78 lakh such persons, 4.18 lakhs are in rural areas and 1.60 lakhs are in cities and towns.

It would be of interest to know if the unemployment, under-employment situation in Karnataka has improved or deteriorated over the past few years. Comparable estimates collected by the National Sample Survey during 1964-65 (19th round) for our State are available. Those estimates are based on the same concept, namely, the number of persons who were seeking work or were available for work and did not get work during the week prior to the data of the survey. They are presented below:

Table X

- **Estimates of Average Number of Persons Total Unemployed in a Week of Different N.S.S. Rounds (in Lakhs)**

	19th ROUND (1964-65)	27th ROUND (1972-73)
Rural	3.56	4.18
Urban	0.57	1.60
Total	4.13	5.78

Between 1964-65 and 1972-73, a period of 8 years, the unemployment–under-employment situation in Karnataka has deteriorated. During this period the population is estimated to have increase by 21.1%, whereas the number of persons seeking work has increased by as much as 40.0%. The number of work seekers has increased from 4.13 lakhs in 1964-65 to 5.78 lakhs in 1972-73. This means that the expansion of employment opportunities has clearly not kept pace with the increase of population. As a result, there has been a continuous addition to the backlog of unemployment— under-employment in the State. While the number of work seekers has increased by 17.4% in rural areas of the State, the number has gone-up by more than three times in urban areas.

The government has taken a few measures to curtail unemployment. Some special schemes to provide productive employment to the rural masses on an ad hoc basis were formulated. Such employment-cum-production oriented special schemes are the Small Farmers Development Agency (SFDA) Marginal Farmers and Agricultural Labourers (MFAL) and Drought Prone Areas Programme (DPAP), but they had only limited coverage. Therefore, a crash scheme for rural employment was introduced. A recent study by the Reserve Bank of India has estimated that the employment generated by the scheme during 1971-72 to 1973-74 in Karnataka was 137.43 lakhs man days of employment. But such schemes have not created a self-sustaining cycle of employment nor enduring assets. The "half-a-million jobs programme for educated unemployed was also similarly abandoned after an year. The fact is that in the Indian circumstances employment is not so much creation of jobs as of work. It has to be understood in the context of enforced idleness under-employment, partial employment and lack of sufficient opportunities for gainful employment.

Thus the major problem remains the growing unemployment. There can be no meaningful development of the economy unless the problem of unemployment and under-employment is treated as the most vital element of planning. Growth, of course, is a must but a faster economic growth does not necessarily lead to larger employment and lopsided growth is not required. What is needed is that kind of growth which creats a vast employment potential in order to absorb the growing population. A large unemployed population constitutes a parasitic burden on those who are engaged in production.

In such a situation, the one important remedy is the control of population. It is now universally recognized in India that the growth of unemployment and the continuing poverty of the people are the direct consequences of the steep rise in population and that population control is a necessary parameters of development.The malaise of educated unemployment which, for obvious reasons, has attracted much greater notice than unemployment and under-employment among the rural population is largely the result of an undesirable pattern of education which is largely unrelated to the economic development of the country. A drastic overhaul of the present educational system and the turn out of graduates of all descriptions on mass production lines must stop. It is believed that wider facilities for technical and professional training should be provided and voca-tionalisation of education would reduce the number of educated unemployed. But it is important that before imparting such training the probable demand for various categories of technical and personnel in different fields of activities is carefully assessed in advance. A purposeful and meaningful manpower planning is required.

Reform of education alone will not solve the problem of middle class unemployment. Economic development nus also proceed in order to catch-up with annual increase in the total working population. The investment rate must be stepped up to the maximum extent as the most important ingradient of employment policy. During the last 25 years of planned development, not much has been achieved in creating employment potential for the new generation. Therefore, investment rate should be such as to accelerate growth in such sectors as would maximize employment opportunities. If rapid industrial development takes place, the middle class would benefit in three ways: (a) the starting of new industries would increase the demand for educated men possessing technical and professional qualifications; (b) as the tempo of industrialization increases, small scale industries will grow and will be linked up with huge factory undertakings and they would absorb a considerable portion; and (c) further industrial development would create new opportunities in the tertiary sector.

Work is one way of placing additional purchasing power in the hands of the poorest in the rural areas. Therefore, employment should become part of an integrated rural development programme for tapping local resources by labour-intensive methods. The needs of the under-employed like farm labour have to be met by creating subsidiary occupations based on agriculature, animal husbandary, fisheries, forestry, piggery and horticulture, apart from other non-agricultural work opportunities. The small and marginal farmers need additional work and income from farming and non-farming sources. The rural artisans and craftmen have to be provided with supporting measures like work places, financial assistance and assured market. It is to be remembered that nothing is more vital for the socio-economic stability and general improvement in the standard of living than implementation of the schemes from the point of view of employment.

The study made of the different facts of the employment—unemployment situation in the country using different measuring tools and examining and collecting the derived results leads us to conclude that the phenomenon is somewhat of the nature of employment-unemployment spectrum having not too large a core of chronically unemployed remaining in cities and towns and partly also in smaller urban pockets, will their exist, centring round the cities and towns, concentric layers of seasonal or short term unemployment and under-employment with varying intensities and acuteness which engulf a large masses of population of different walks of life.

Any programme of action for taking off the country from the unemployment and underemployment and under-employment rut, should consequently be multi-pronged with emphasis, of course, on agriculture and in other rural-works-programme. If increasing demand for labour can be created in the country side the steams of following population in search of job and work to the urban areas can be arrested and the tendency of the hard core of unemployment getting still harder can be stopped.

Table I

· **Percentage of Population in Urban Labour Force-Employment and Unemployment: Karnataka**

SI. NO.	PERIOD OF SURVEY	PERCENTAGE OF LABOUR FORCE	EMPLOYMENT	UNEMPLOYMENT
1	July 1958 to June 1959	35.02	33.91	1.11
2	Feb. 1963 to Jan. 1964	27.74	27.28	0.46
3	July 1964 to June 1965	27.00	26.99	0.01

Table II (a)

- Percentage of Males in Urban Labour Force Employment and Unemployment: Karnataka

Sl. NO.	PERIOD OF SURVEY	PERCENTAGE OF LABOUR FORCE	EMPLOYMENT	UNEMPLOYMENT
1	July 1958 to June 1959	49.02	47.39	1.63
2	Feb. 1963 to Jan. 1964	46.77	46.03	0.74
3	July 1964 to June 1965	44.91	44.90	0.01

- **Source:**

- G.O.I., National Sample Survey, Sl. No. (1) 14th round of N.S.S., July 1958 to June 1959, Department of Statistics, p.8.

- G.O.I., National Sample Survey, Sl. No. (2) and (3) 18th round and 19th round of N.S.S.-Department of Statistics, p.9.

Table II (b)

- Percentage of Females in Urban Labour Force Employment and Unemployment: Karnataka

Sl. NO.	PERIOD OF SURVEY	PERCENTAGE OF LABOUR FORCE	EMPLOYMENT	UNEMPLOYMENT
1	July 1958 to June 1959	21.03	20.43	0.60
2	Feb. 1963 to Jan. 1964	7.42	7.26	0.16
3	July 1964 to June 1965	27.32	27.32	0.00

- Source:

- 1. G.O.I., National Sample Survey, Sl. No. (1) 14th round of N.S.S. For Sl. No. (2) and (3) 18th round and 19th round N.S.S., Department of Statistics, p.10.

Table III

Percentage Distribution of Persons in Karnataka State in each Age Group by Activity Status—Urban—18th Round of N.S.S. (January 1963 to February 1964)

SI. NO	AGE GROUP	PERSONS IN LABOUR FORCE			PERSONS NOT IN LABOUR FORCE	NOT RECORDED
		GAINFULLY EMPLOYED	UNEMPLOYED	TOTAL		
1	0-14	1.20	0.03	1.23	98.77	-
2	15-19	23.09	0.85	23.94	76.06	-
3	20-24	36.72	2.24	38.96	61.04	-
4	25-29	1.06	47.94	49.00	51.00	-
5	30-39	61.56	0.27	61.83	38.17	-
6	40-49	61.71	0.43	62.14	37.46	-
7	50-59	44.89	0.24	45.13	54.87	-
8	60+	23.36	-	23.36	76.64	-
Total		27.29	0.46	27.75	72.25	-

• Source : G.O.I., National Sample Survey, 18th round of N.S.S. (January 1963 to February 1964), Department of Statistics, p.11.

Table IV

- Percentage Distribution of Persons in Karnataka State in each Age Group by Activity Status— Urban—18th Round of N.S.S. (January 1963 to February 1964)

SI. No.	Age group	PERSONS IN LABOUR FORCE			Persons not in labour force	Not recorded
		Gainfully employed	Unemployed	Total		
1	0-14	2.03	0.06	2.09	97.91	-
2	15-19	36.68	1.00	37.68	62.32	-
3	20-24	71.95	4.29	76.24	23.76	-
4	25-29	91.44	2.39	93.83	6.76	-
5	30-39	96.13	0.32	96.45	3.55	-
6	40-49	95.21	0.50	95.71	4.29	-
7	50-59	78.42	0.53	78.95	21.05	-
8	60+	43.82	-	43.82	56.19	-
Total		46.03	0.74	46.77	53.23	-

- Source : G.O.I., National Sample Survey, 18[r]h round of N.S.S. (January 1963 to February 1964), Department of Statistics, p.12.

Table V

- Percentage Distribution of Male in Karnataka State in each Age Group by Activity Status—Urban—18th Round of N.S.S. (January 1963 to February 1964)

Sl. No.	Age group	PERSONS IN LABOUR FORCE			Persons not in labour force	Not recorded
		Gainfully employed	Unemployed	Total		
1	0-14	0.32	-	0.32	99.68	-
2	15-19	5.77	0.64	6.41	93.59	-
3	20-24	7.63	0.54	8.17	91.83	-
4	25-29	12.94	-	12.94	87.06	-
5	30-39	19.56	0.21	16.77	83.23	-
6	40-49	17.82	0.33	18.15	81.25	-
7	50-59	17.32	-	17.32	82.68	-
8	60+	2.31	-	2.31	97.69	-
Total		7.25	0.16	7.41	92.59	-

- Source: G.O.I., National Sample Survey, 18th round of N.S.S. (January 1963 to February 1964), Department of Statistics, p.13.

Table VI

- Number of 'Unemployed' persons of Age 15-59 According to 'Weekly Activity' Status and 'Daily Activity' Status for All-India* (in lakhs)

All Subrounds Combined	NUMBER OF PERSONS UNEMPLOYED ACCORDING TO:		
	WEEKLY ACTIVITY		DAILY ACTIVITY
	Male	Female	Male
Rural	45.2	22.0	85.5
	(2.51)	(1.72)	(6.67)
Urban	23.5	8.8	30.2
	(6.23)	(2.66)	(8.00)

- *The figure in brackets give the percentage of persons 'unemployed' to total population of age 15-59.

- Source : G.O.I., National Sample Survey, Report No. 298, Report on the second quinquennial Survery on employment and unemployment, 32nd round (July 1977—June 1978), Director of Statistics, 1981, Delhi, p.13.

Table VII

- Daily Status Unemployment Rates by Household Expenditure Group, N.S.S. 27th Round, 1972-73, Rural India

SI. NO.	HOUSEHOLD EXPENDITURE GROUP (RUPEES PER HEAD PER MONTH)	UNEMPLOYMENT RATE (PERCENT)
1	0-10.99	22.42
2	11-20.99	14.08

3	21-33.99	9.82
4	34-54.99	7.12
5	55-99.99	5.18
6	100 and over	2.33
7	All including unrecorded	8.24

• Source: G.O.I., National Sample Survey, 27th round, Report No. 255/10, p.46.

• Note: Person days outside the labour force of persons in the weekly labour force have been excluded from the denominator, which gives the daily status labour force.

Table VIII

• Unemployment Rates by States (percent)

Sl. NO.	STATES	UNEMPLOYMENT RATE
1	Kerala	26.02
2	Tamil Nadu	16.06
3	Andhra Pradesh	10.78
4	West Bengal	10.44
5	Karnataka	9.58
6	Orissa	8.16
7	Maharashtra	8.15

8	Bihar	8.13
9	Haryana	6.87
10	Gujarat	6.38
11	Chandigarh	5.55
12	Punjab	5.03
13	Uttar Pradesh	4.29
14	Rajasthan	3.55
15	Madhya Pradesh	3.13
16	Himachal Pradesh	2.19
17	Meghalaya	2.5
18	Assam	1.82
19	Nagaland	0.52
20	Manipur	N.A.
21	Tripura	N.A.
22	Arunachal Pradesh	N.A.
23	Mizoram	N.A.

Table IX

- Per cent of Unemployed to Persons in labour Force for Population of Age 15-59 on the Basis of 'Weekly Activity' and 'Daily Activity' Status

STATES/ UNION TERRITORY		WEEKLY ACTIVITY				DAILY ACTIVITY		
		RURAL		URBAN		RURAL		URBAN
		Male	Female	Male	Female	Male	Female	Male
All India		3.89	4.39	7.35	11.94	7.56	9.51	9.54
1	Andhra Pradesh	4.26	8.50	8.20	11.90	8.66	14.32	10.73
2	Assam	1.61	0.92	4.14	10.96	1.59	1.20	3.92
3	Bihar	4.56	4.73	6.82	9.01	7.77	9.70	8.14
4	Gujarat	2.96	2.34	5.09	5.86	6.35	5.69	6.98
5	Haryana	5.07	1.37	5.66	7.91	7.61	3.02	7.06
6	Himachal Pradesh	1.99	-	5.71	12.03	2.91	0.15	6.25
7	Jammu and Kashmir	4.23	1.73	4.65	17.49	6.42	2.40	5.24
8	Karnataka	3.12	4.63	6.97	9.15	8.35	11.42	10.59
9	Kerala	12.96	13.63	15.33	16.06	25.99	28.94	25.16

10	Madhya Pradesh	1.41	1.86	4.87	4.31	2.44	3.32	5.85
11	Maharashtra	3.03	4.14	7.76	15.83	6.16	9.21	9.07
12	Meghalaya	-	-	1.28	7.5	-	-	1.04
13	Nagaland	-	-	0.60	-	-	-	0.60
14	Orissa	4.08	5.62	6.99	8.23	7.82	9.38	8.67
15	Punjab	2.82	1.05	3.93	8.13	5.46	2.18	4.88
16	Rajasthan	2.45	1.59	4.60	1.60	3.49	2.24	5.69
17	Tamil Nadu	6.19	5.50	9.47	13.92	15.80	17.77	14.12
18	Uttar Pradesh	2.73	1.25	5.23	4.15	4.28	2.75	6.71
19	West Bengal	4.75	3.88	9.93	14.13	9.66	10.28	11.85
20	Chandigarh	-	-	2.29	16.28	-	-	2.86
21	Delhi	8.70	20.92	6.87	31.48	9.38	28.87	7.35
22	Goa, Daman & Diu	11.20	12.12	10.63	12.97	15.51	14.03	12.07
23	Pondicherry	10.47	7.53	14.18	13.45	27.08	25.11	17.90

• Source: N.S.S. op. cit., pp. 16-19.

Table X

• Percentage of Persons Seeking and Available for Work

SI. NO.	STATES	RURAL			URBAN	
		MALE	FEMALE	TOTAL	MALE	FEMALE
1	Andhra Pradesh	0.46	0.10	0.28	3.91	1.73
2	Assam	0.66	0.23	0.46	2.26	0.44
3	Bihar	1.37	0.28	0.82	3.01	0.45
4	Gujarat	0.60	0.10	0.36	1.60	0.43
5	Haryana	0.93	0.07	0.52	2.39	0.96
6	Jammu and Kashmir	0.23	0.09	0.16	1.38	0.33
7	Karnataka	0.59	0.16	0.38	2.93	0.86
8	Kerala	3.34	1.58	2.43	6.41	3.47
9	Madhya Pradesh	0.09	-	0.05	2.99	0.68
10	Maharashtra	0.51	0.07	0.28	2.72	1.13
11	Orissa	0.91	0.18	0.54	3.26	0.91
12	Punjab	0.57	0.05	0.33	1.95	1.13
13	Rajasthan	0.53	0.28	0.41	1.12	0.42
14	Tamil Nadu	0.99	0.22	0.60	3.89	1.08
15	Uttar Pradesh	0.41	0.09	0.26	1.44	0.21
16	West Bengal	1.22	0.54	0.89	4.86	1.78
	All India	0.79	0.23	052	2.90	1.07

• Source: G.O.I., National Sample Survey, 27th round 1972-73, No. 225-A, Department of Statistics, April 1976, Delhi, p. 16.

Table XI

- Percentage of Persons in Labour Force to Total Population of Age 15-59 on the Basis of "Weekly" Activity and "Daily Activity"(All sub-rounds combined)

	STATES / UNION TERRITORY	URBAN		RURAL		RURAL		URBAN
		Male	Female	Male	Female	Male	Female	Male
1	Andhra Pradesh	93.04	57.83	86.34	29.86	90.33	53.68	84.83
2	Assam	88.27	12.03	81.60	7.77	82.34	10.35	79.15
3	Bihar	91.03	24.50	83.64	14.18	89.64	22.65	83.20
4	Gujarat	90.30	51.01	84.50	18.79	88.32	40.91	83.91
5	Haryana	89.08	26.79	84.88	17.40	87.82	18.71	84.25
6	Himachal Pradesh	88.93	62.05	84.35	22.96	86.09	49.33	84.03
7	Jammu and Kashmir	91.30	25.26	83.14	13.13	90.04	18.99	82.87
8	Karnataka	91.33	49.35	82.31	25.53	88.77	43.63	81.78
9	Kerala	82.66	39.48	82.61	30.80	78.69	32.72	79.74
10	Madhya Pradesh	92.05	53.68	83.11	19.67	90.03	48.77	81.30
11	Maharashtra	90.57	62.11	83.88	24.59	88.11	56.44	83.29
12	Meghalaya	-	-	77.08	29.87	-	-	75.89

13	Nagaland	-	-	85.71	19.83	-	-	85.71
14	Orissa	91.27	29.96	83.09	20.73	88.22	26.63	82.00
15	Punjab	88.24	28.51	86.29	16.98	86.37	19.14	85.22
16	Rajasthan	91.53	53.06	81.35	18.72	89.88	46.04	80.60
17	Tamil Nadu	91.21	53.54	88.91	35.31	88.10	47.78	87.60
18	Uttar Pradesh	89.60	26.38	84.12	13.25	88.03	22.88	83.09
19	West Bengal	90.91	16.17	87.17	15.18	89.44	14.60	86.36
20	Chandigarh	-	-	80.74	17.57	-	-	80.74
21	Delhi	84.15	14.28	88.47	20.38	84.15	10.35	85.07
22	Goa, Daman & Diu	81.10	53.07	76.98	38.68	80.17	47.98	75.87
23	Pondicherry	86.37	31.03	81.64	17.05	83.27	24.36	81.02
	All India	90.44	39.32	84.74	22.18	88.20	34.67	88.83

• Source: G.O.I., "Sarvekshana", Journal of the National Sample Survey Organisation, Vol. II, No. 4, April 1979, Department of Statistics, Ministry of Planning, 1980, Delhi.

Labour Participation Rates (Percentages) by Sex and Rural/Urban

Sl. NO.	STATES	RURAL			URBAN		
		MALE	FEMALE	TOTAL	MALE	FEMALE	
1	Andhra Pradesh	72.64	51.07	61.88	60.65	23.04	
2	Assam	58.88	9.95	35.52	58.88	6.01	

3	Bihar	62.46	23.62	42.87	58.27	11.36
4	Gujarat	61.97	43.37	53.05	55.39	15.51
5	Haryana	58.42	35.98	47.70	57.52	11.83
6	Jammu and Kashmir	62.12	26.36	44.53	56.71	7.16
7	Karnataka	67.05	49.74	58.64	58.14	19.32
8	Kerala	57.73	29.73	43.22	57.18	25.26
9	Madhya Pradesh	67.27	52.73	60.24	55.23	18.43
10	Maharashtra	64.66	45.67	54.44	61.40	17.85
11	Orissa	67.46	30.85	49.05	62.59	18.82
12	Punjab	64.22	32.23	48.33	60.90	15.43
13	Rajasthan	69.41	63.09	66.37	55.22	23.53
14	Tamil Nadu	70.23	51.33	60.69	61.98	19.77
15	Uttar Pradesh	63.29	31.57	48.13	59.32	9.60
16	West Bengal	61.17	15.87	39.19	64.72	11.61
	All India	64.80	37.35	51.23	59.64	16.56

• **Source: G.O.I., National Sample Survey, 27th round, p. 17.**

Table XIII

• Percent age of Working Persons to Total Population of Age 15-59 on the basis of "Weekly Activity" and "Daily Activity"

STATES/ UNION TERRITORY		RURAL		URBAN		RURAL		URBAN
		MALE	FEMALE	MALE	FEMALE	MALE	FEMALE	MALE
All India		86.92	37.60	78.55	19.55	81.52	31.37	75.84
1	Andhra Pradesh	89.07	52.91	79.26	26.30	82.51	45.99	75.73
2	Assam	86.85	11.92	78.22	6.92	81.03	10.23	76.05
3	Bihar	86.88	23.34	77.94	12.90	82.68	20.45	76.43
4	Gujarat	87.62	49.82	80.20	17.69	82.72	38.58	78.05
5	Haryana	84.56	26.42	80.08	16.02	81.14	18.15	78.30
6	Himachal Pradesh	87.16	62.05	79.54	20.20	83.59	49.25	78.77
7	Jammu and Kashmir	87.44	24.82	79.27	10.83	84.26	18.53	78.53
8	Karnataka	88.48	47.06	76.58	23.80	81.36	38.65	72.67
9	Kerala	72.94	34.01	69.94	25.86	58.22	23.25	59.68
10	Madhya Pradesh	90.75	52.69	78.11	18.82	87.84	47.16	76.55
11	Maharashtra	87.82	59.54	77.38	20.70	82.68	51.24	75.74

12	Meghalaya	-	-	76.09	27.70	-	-	75.10
13	Nagaland	-	-	85.20	19.83	-	-	85.20
14	Orissa	87.54	28.28	77.28	19.02	81.32	24.14	74.89
15	Punjab	85.76	28.21	82.90	15.49	81.65	18.72	81.06
16	Rajasthan	89.29	52.22	77.61	18.42	86.74	45.01	76.01
17	Tamil Nadu	85.57	50.59	80.49	30.39	74.18	39.29	75.23
18	Uttar Pradesh	87.15	26.05	79.71	12.70	84.26	22.25	77.51
19	West Bengal	86.60	15.54	78.51	13.04	80.79	13.10	76.12
20	Chandigarh	-	-	78.89	14.71	-	-	78.43
21	Delhi	76.83	14.58	79.60	13.96	76.25	9.5	78.81
22	Goa, Daman & Diu	71.93	46.63	68.79	38.66	67.73	41.25	66.71
23	Pondicherry	77.32	28.70	70.06	14.76	60.72	18.24	66.51

• **Source: G.O.I., N.S.S. op. cit., p. 10.**

Table XIV

- Percentage of People Seeking and Available for Work to Total Labour Force

SI. NO.	STATES	RURAL			URBAN	
		Male	Female	Total	Male	Female
1	Andhra Pradesh	0.63	0.20	0.45	6.45	7.51
2	Assam	1.12	2.31	1.30	3.84	7.32
3	Bihar	2.19	1.19	1.91	5.11	3.96
4	Gujarat	0.97	0.23	0.68	2.89	2.77
5	Haryana	1.59	0.19	1.09	4.16	8.44
6	Jammu and Kashmir	0.37	0.34	0.36	2.43	4.65
7	Karnataka	0.88	0.32	0.65	5.04	4.45
8	Kerala	5.79	5.31	5.62	11.21	13.58
9	Madhya Pradesh	0.13	-	0.08	3.97	3.69
10	Maharashtra	0.79	0.15	0.51	4.43	6.33
11	Orissa	1.35	0.58	1.10	5.21	4.98
12	Punjab	0.89	0.17	0.68	3.20	7.32
13	Rajasthan	0.76	0.44	0.62	2.19	1.78
14	Tamil Nadu	1.41	0.43	0.99	6.28	5.46
15	Uttar Pradesh	0.65	0.28	0.54	2.03	2.19

16	West Bengal	1.99	3.40	2.27	7.51	15.33
	All India	1.22	0.63	1.01	4.86	6.47

• **Source: N.S.S., op. cit., p. 18.**

Table XV

• Percentage of Seeking and Available for Work Person.

		WEEK BY CURRENT ACTIVITY STATUS				
		RURAL			URBAN	
SI. NO.	STATES	MALE	FEMALE	TOTAL	MALE	FEMALE
1	Andhra Pradesh	2.02	3.97	2.98	4.74	2.52
2	Assam	0.82	0.19	0.53	1.36	0.27
3	Bihar	2.46	1.82	2.16	3.58	1.02
4	Gujarat	1.30	0.87	1.11	2.11	0.37
5	Haryana	1.20	0.25	0.75	3.29	1.07
6	Jammu and Kashmir	8.84	0.64	4.78	2.66	0.64
7	Karnataka	1.79	2.50	2.13	3.80	1.16
8	Kerala	6.04	4.35	5.16	8.17	4.20
9	Madhya Pradesh	0.88	1.20	1.06	2.00	0.89
10	Maharashtra	1.65	1.76	1.70	3.33	1.55

11	Orissa	2.13	2.50	2.30	2.77	1.55
12	Punjab	1.28	0.32	0.84	2.58	1.35
13	Rajasthan	3.22	1.89	2.58	2.43	0.82
14	Tamil Nadu	2.36	1.65	2.01	4.43	1.72
15	Uttar Pradesh	0.89	0.69	0.80	1.67	0.27
16	West Bengal	1.66	1.28	1.46	5.16	1.71
	All India	1.86	1.73	1.80	3.38	1.40

• Source : N.S.S., op. cit., p. 20.

Table XVI

• Percentage of Person-Days Seeking and Available to Total Labour Force Peron-days in a Week

SI. NO.	STATES	RURAL			URBAN		
		MALE	FEMALE	TOTAL	MALE	FEMALE
1	Andhra Pradesh	6.43	14.72	9.61	10.88	16.89
2	Assam	2.23	2.42	2.25	3.28	5.26
3	Bihar	8.85	13.83	10.17	7.62	14.00
4	Gujarat	6.42	5.51	6.08	6.54	5.50
5	Haryana	3.33	1.06	2.52	7.65	11.68
6	Jammu and Kashmir	17.17	5.39	14.36	5.99	11.52

7	Karnataka	7.40	11.62	9.04	8.41	7.67
8	Kerala	22.96	26.76	24.26	22.99	24.10
9	Madhya Pradesh	2.38	3.83	2.98	4.11	6.35
10	Maharashtra	7.21	10.53	8.64	7.48	12.44
11	Orissa	7.06	14.84	9.32	5.76	13.12
12	Punjab	4.40	1.87	3.67	5.96	8.91
13	Rajasthan	5.32	3.24	4.41	5.11	4.55
14	Tamil Nadu	9.38	12.56	10.63	9.78	14.20
15	Uttar Pradesh	2.98	3.37	3.11	4.34	3.31
16	West Bengal	8.45	14.52	9.55	9.62	17.32
	All India	6.57	9.20	7.48	7.70	12.03

• **Source: N.S.S., op. cit., p. 22.**

Table XVII

• The 'Rates of Under-utilisation' of 'Working Persons' of Age 15-59 by Sex and Resident Status

Sl. NO.	STATES/UNION TERRITORIES	RURAL		URBAN
		Male	Female	Male
1	All India	6.21	16.57	3.45
2	Andhra Pradesh	7.36	13.08	4.45
3	Assam	6.70	14.18	2.77

4	Bihar	4.83	12.38	1.94
5	Gujarat	5.59	22.56	2.68
6	Haryana	4.04	31.30	2.22
7	Himachal Pradesh	4.10	20.63	0.77
8	Jammu and Kashmir	3.64	25.34	0.93
9	Karnataka	8.05	17.87	5.11
10	Kerala	19.07	31.82	14.97
11	Madhya Pradesh	3.21	10.50	2.00
12	Maharashtra	5.85	13.94	2.12
13	Meghalaya	-	-	1.30
14	Nagaland	-	-	0.00
15	Orissa	7.11	14.64	3.09
16	Punjab	4.79	33.64	2.22
17	Rajasthan	2.86	13.81	2.06
18	Tamil Nadu	13.31	22.34	6.53
19	Uttar Pradesh	3.32	14.59	2.76
20	West Bengal	6.71	15.70	3.04
21	Chandigarh	-	-	0.58
22	Delhi	0.75	34.84	0.99
23	Goa, Daman & Diu	5.84	11.54	3.02
24	Pondicherry	21.47	36.45	5.07

• **Source: N.S.S., op. cit., p. 11.**

Table XVIII

- Unemployment in Equivalent Person-YearsUnemployment Rate Per Sq. kms and the Shares of States to All-India

SL. NO.	STATES/UNION TERRITORY	UNEMPLOYMENT IN EQUIVALENT PERSON-YEARS (MILLION)	UNEMPLOYMENT IN EQUIVALENT PERSON-YEAR PER SQ. KMS.	SHARE OF STATE IN ALL INDIA UNEMPLOYMENT (%)
1	Kerala	1.88	48.21	10.11
2	West Bengal	1.64	18.64	8.79
3	Tamil Nadu	2.35	18.08	12.63
4	Bihar	2.05	11.78	11.05
5	Andhra Pradesh	2.32	8.38	12.49
6	Maharashtra	2.22	7.21	11.93
7	Orissa	1.01	6.47	5.43
8	Karnataka	1.18	6.15	6.36
9	Punjab	9.23	4.60	1.26
10	Uttar Pradesh	1.22	4.15	6.54
11	Tripura	0.04	4.00	0.19
12	Haryana	0.15	3.41	3.56
13	Gujarat	0.66	3.37	3.85
14	Madhya Pradesh	0.71	1.60	2.62
15	Rajasthan	0.49	1.43	0.48
16	Assam	0.09	1.14	0.41

17	Manipur	0.02	0.91	0.74
18	Jammu & Kashmir	0.14	0.63	0.05
19	Meghalaya	0.01	0.45	0.01
20	Nagaland	Less than 0.0005	0.29	Less than 0.06
21	Himachal Pradesh	0.01	Less than 0.18	
	India	18.57	5.65	100.00

• **Source: op, cit.**

Table XIX

State-wise Distribution of Population and Labour Force Participation Rates

SI. NO.	STATES/ UNION TERRITORIES	POPULATION GROWTH (LAKHS) 1961-71	LABOUR PARTICIPATION RATION 1971	LABOUR FORCE GROWTH (LAKHS)	ANNUAL LABOR FORCE GROWTH (LAKHS)	ANNUAL PER SQ. KM GROWTH
1	Andhra Pradesh	75.19	41.38	31.11	3.1	1.12
2	Assam	77.08	28.08	21.64	2.2	2.74
3	Bihar	99.06	31.03	30.74	3.1	1.77
4	Haryana	24.46	31.46	7.75	0.7	0.40
5	Himachal Pradesh	30.94	37.14	11.49	1.1	2.05
6	Jammu and Kashmir	10.56	30.43	3.21	0.3	0.15

7	Karnataka	57.12	34.81	19.88	2.0	1.04
8	Kerala	44.44	29.11	12.94	1.3	3.32
9	Madhya Pradesh	92.82	36.69	34.06	3.4	0.77
10	Maharashtra	108.59	36.51	39.65	4.0	1.29
11	Manipur	2.93	36.36	1.07	0.1	0.49
12	Meghalaya	2.42	50.00	1.21	0.1	0.85
13	Nagaland	1.47	60.00	0.88	0.08	0.55
14	Orissa	43.96	31.51	13.85	1.3	0.89
15	Punjab	12.44	27.00	3.36	0.3	0.67
16	Rajasthan	56.10	31.40	17.62	1.8	0.02
17	Tamil Nadu	75.12	35.68	26.80	2.7	2.06
18	Tripura	4.14	25.00	1.04	0.1	1.04
19	Uttar Pradesh	145.87	30.92	45.10	4.5	1.53
20	West Bengal	93.86	27.99	26.27	2.6	2.99
	All India	1089.25	32.91	358.47	35.8	1.09

• **Source: op. cit.**

Table XX

· **Percentage of Population Below Poverty Line**

SI. NO.	STATES	POVERTY RATION %
1	Orissa	67.50
2	Bihar	64.06
3	West Bengal	62.28
4	Kerala	62.25
5	Tamil Nadu	60.71
6	Madhya Pradesh	57.50
7	Uttar Pradesh	50.38
8	Karnataka	49.44
9	Andhra Pradesh	47.85
10	Gujarat	44.58
11	Maharashtra	43.99
12	Rajasthan	43.50
13	Assam	32.95
14	Haryana	32.24
15	Punjab	21.62

• Source: G.O.I., Reports of the Finance Commission, 1978, p. 80.

Table XXI

- Distribution of Person-Weeks (Age Group 15-59) and Person-days (Age Group 15-59) by Current Activity Status Category, Sex and Resident Status (Rural / Urban)

Current Category	Activity	Status	RURAL ESTIMATED NUMBER (IN 00) OF				URBAN ESTIMATED NUMBER (IN 00) OF		
			Person-Weeks		Person-Days		Person-weeks		Person-days
			Male	Female	Male	Female	Male	Female	Male
1			2	3	4	5	6	7	8
1	Bonded Labour (01-04)		2979	398	2837	361	65	8	66
2	Self-Employed (Including Helper)	A	575081	244100	559760	210648	15672	7805	15289
		B	127943	44479	122845	38364	99062	20713	96784
		T	703024	288579	682605	249012	114734	28518	112073
3	Regular Salaried/ Paid Employees	A	48339	6797	47354	6230	2565	645	2640
		B	76757	19415	76529	11771	1439006	19809	143390
		T	125096	19212	123883	18001	146471	20454	145994

4	Casual Labor in Public Works		9211	4058	8112	3384	1158	304	989
5	Casual labour in other types of work	A	229386	149720	191975	115766	7749	6552	5997
		B	48280	17702	39126	13736	26168	8765	20999
		T	277666	167422	231101	129502	33917	15317	26996
6	Total working		1117976	479669	1048538	400260	296345	64601	286118
7	Seeking work		32489	12439	55761	23304	20518	6558	24693
8	Not seeking work but available for work		12769	9592	30051	18739	3003	2198	5470
9	Total un-employed		45258	22031	85812	42043	23521	8756	30163
10	Total labour force		1163234	501700	1134350	442303	319866	73357	316281
11	Students		66710	16435	67395	16809	44619	25505	44805
12	Engaged in domestic duties		5649	437903	14833	472248	1264	183454	2445
13	Engaged in domestic duties and also free collection		24622	266065	7735	285911	211	38085	300

14	Others not in labour force	36919	47381	49562	50704	10251	9659	11897
15	Casual labour abstained from work due to sickness	9015	6300	12274	7809	1069	596	1652
16	Total not in labour force	122915	774084	151799	833481	57414	257299	60999
17	Total	1286149			1275784	377280	330656	377280

- * Excludes Sukir Hills and North Cochar Hills of Assam, Arunachal Pradesh, Meghalaya, Mizo-ram, Manipur and Tripura as sub-round estimates are not available.

- ** Excludes Manipur, Tripura, Arunachal Pradesh as data not available for tabulation.Source: op. cit., p. 24.

- Distribution of Person-Weeks (Age Group 15-59) and Person-days (Age Group 15-59) by Current Activity Status Category, Sex and Resident Status (Rural / Urban)

ALL INDIA			RURAL ESTIMATED NUMBER (IN 00) OF				URBAN ESTIMATED NUMBER (IN 00) OF		
			Person-Weeks		Person-Days		Person-weeks		Person-days
Current Category	Activity	Status	Male	Female	Male	Female	Male	Female	Male

1			2	3	4	5	6	7	8
1	Bonded Labour (01-04)		94	41	92	40	6	-	6
2	Self-Employed	A	28964	12679	28011	11046	1315	507	1274
		B	5253	2074	5105	1837	5537	1413	5329
		T	34217	14753	33116	12883	6852	1950	6603
3	Regular Salaried/Paid Employees	A	2092	400	2064	393	195	12	248
		B	2999	248	2988	243	7575	1248	7493
		T	5091	648	5052	636	7770	1260	7741
4	Casual Labor in Public Works		436	201	503	181	139	6	106
5	Casual labour in other types of work	A	19295	12013	13319	9079	772	744	631
		B	3083	1976	2371	1514	2596	1095	2122
		T	19378	13989	15690	10593	3368	1839	2753
6	Total working		59216	29632	54453	24333	18135	5055	17209
7	Seeking work		1076	673	2385	1580	1132	342	1479
8	Not seeking work but available for work		830	766	2573	1556	226	167	559
9	Total unemployed		1906	1439	4958	31136	1358	509	2038
10	Total labour force		61122	31071	59411	27469	19493	5564	19247
11	Students		2521	690	2535	720	3105	1640	3113

12	Engaged in domestic duties		380	21183	1185	23668	155	12645	265
13	Engaged in domestic duties and also free collection		121	6737	177	7485	26	1122	37
14	Others not in labour force		2049	2490	2663	2659	783	725	858
15	Casual labour abstained from work due to sickness		733	791	955	961	119	94	161
16	Total not in labour force		5804	31891	7515	35493	4188	16226	4434
17	Total		66926	62962	66926	62962	23681	21790	23681

• Source: op. cit., p. 24.

BIBLIOGRAPHY

Ahluwalia, Montek S., (et al.): Grwoth and poverty in Developing Countries, World Bank Staff Working Paper No.: 309, Washington D.C., December 1978.

Arshad Mohamad: "Poverty and Levels of Living in India", Southern Economist, Vol. 17, No. 8, August 15, 1978.

Dandekar, Kumudini: "Tackling of Unemployment Problems through Employment Guarantee", Joint Conference, International Economic Association and Indian Economic Association, Pune, March 16-24, 1980.

Dantwala, M.L.,: Notes on some aspects of Rural Employment, Indian Journal of Agricultural Economics, Vol. VIII, No.2.

Hall Robert E.: Is Unemployment a Macro Economic Problem, American Economic Review, Vol. 73, No.2, Mar. 1983, pp.219-222.

Hanumantha, Rayappa and Deepak Grover: Employment Planning for the Rural Poor: The case of Scheduled Caste and Scheduled Tribes, Sterling Publishers Pvt. Ltd., New Delhi 1980.

Krishna Raj: Unemployment in India. Economic and Politicial Weekly, Vol. VIII, No.9.

Little, I.M.D.,: A Critical Examination of India's Third Year Plan, Oxford Economic papers, Vol. 14, No. 1, Feb-1962, p.24.

Mahalanobis, P.C.,: Science and National Planning, Sankhya, Vol. 20, Parts 1 & 2, Sept. 1958, pp. 77-78.

Mehrau Farhad: Employment Data for the Measurement of Living Standard, World Bank, Working Paper, Washington D.C., October 1980.

Mydral Gunnar: An Approach to the Asian Drama, New York, Vintage Books, 1970.

Nanjundappa, D.M., and Srinivasa, M.A.: "Employment and Unemployment in Karnataka", paper presented at Joint Conference of International Economic Association and Indian Economic Association, Pune, March 16-24, 1980.

Prabhakara, N.R and M N Usha: Population Growth and Unemployment in India; Asish Publishing House, New Delhi (1986).

N R Prabhakara; Population Growth and Unemployment in India by Caste: Path Analysis; America Star Books, Baltimore, USA (2014).

Puri, M.M.K.: Poverty and Planning in India Handicaps and Challenges, Southern Economist, Vol. 23, No. 3, June 1984, pp. 9-10.

Rao, V.K.R.V.: Inter-State Variations in Population Growth and Population Policy, Vol. 16, No. 51, Dec. 19, 1981, Economic and Political weekly, pp. 2105-81.

Rao, V.K.R.V. (ed): Planning in Perspective Policy Choices in Planning for Karnataka 1974-74 to 1988-89, New Delhi, Allied Publishers, 1978.

Rao, V.K.R.V.: Planning for Change: Issues in Mysore's Development, Vikas Publishing House, Delhi 1975.

Rao, V.K.R.V.: Food, Nutrition and Poverty in India, Vikas Publishing House Pvt. Ltd., New Delhi, 1982.

Rao, V.G. and Mishjra, G.P.: Rural Poverty Growth and Determinants, I.S.E.C., Bangalore, 1980, (Mimeo)

Robinson Joan: Disguised Unemployment, Economic Journal, XLVI, No. 182 June, 1936, pp. 225.

Singh, Tarlok: Decade for Ending Rural Poverty, Seminar, No. 282, Feb. 1983, pp. 14-19.

Subramanyam, S.: Unemployment in India: A Review, Indian Journal of Labor Economics, Vol. 26, No.3, Oct. 1983, pp. 237-256.

Sukhatme, P.V.: Where in Poverty Line? Economic Scene, Aug. 1, 1983, pp. 58-59.

Turnham, D. and Jaegan, I: The Employment Problem in Less Development Countries, A Review of Evidence Paris, OECD, 1971.

United Nations: Poverty, Unemployment and Development Policy: A Case Study of Selected Issues with reference to Kerala, ST/ESA/29, New York, 1975.

Visaria, P.M., and Visaria, L.: Employment Planning for Weaker Sections in Rural India, Economic and Political Weekly, Vol. XIII, No. 4-6, 1973.

Vorieo Barend Ade: Public Policy and Private Sector; Economic Development and the Private Sector: Finance Development, Washington, IMF and World Bank, 1981.

• PRABHAKARA R. NARASANDRA

- Author has D Lit, From Tumkur University for the thesis "The Economic Activity of Children and Child Labor in India: Issues and Concerns".

- Master of Science in Statistics: Bangalore University, India and studied in California State University, Fullerton. June 1992.

- Master's Thesis: Preference for Sons, Its Impact on Fertility: An Empirical Study on India.

RELATED COURSES:

- Applied Sociology

- Social Statistics

- Advanced Theory of Urban Sociology

- Advanced Survey Research

- Research Methodology

WORK EXPERIENCE:

- Research Assistant June 1974- Jan 1989 Population Research Center, Institute For Social And Economic Change, Bangalore, India.

- Teaching Assistant Math Dept. UCI, California.

PUBLICATION: BOOKS:

1. Population Growth and Unemployment in India.

   - Ashish Publishing House, New Delhi, 1986.

2. Internal Migration and Population Redistribution in India.

   - Concept Publishing Company, New Delhi, 1986.

3. Preference for Sons, Its Impact On fertility: An Empirical Study on India. Publish America, 2012. USA.

4. Population Growth Of Asian and Pacific Islanders In California: Causes and Consequences: Publish America, 2012.

5. Urbanism and Quality of Life: Some Reflections: America Star Books, Baltimore, USA, 20146

6. Population Growth and Unemployment in India by Caste: Path Analysis; America Star Books, Baltimore, 2014.

7. Population Education; APH Publishing Corporation, New Delhi, 2028.

8. Sex Composition of the Population and Fertility Transition in India. A.P.H Publishing House, New Delhi, India, 2020.

9. Child Migration and Child Labor; A.P.H. Publishing Corporation, New Delhi, India 2020.

10. Trends in Population Growth and Unemployment in India by Caste: Some Reflections; APH Publishing Corporation; New Delhi, India;2021.

RESEARCH PAPERS:

1. Patterns Of Child Migration And Child Migrant Lab our in The Cities Of India; Santayana, 1984,2(1), pp. 19-28.

2. The Patterns of Rural-Urban Internal Migration: Its Socio-Economic Correlates Indian Journal of Lab our Economics, 1984, Vol. XXVI, No.4 Jan, pp313-330

3. Patterns of Population Growth in Southern States; Economic And Political Weekly, Vol. 18. No. 48, pp. 2018.

4. Migration and Economic Influence: Child Migrant in India; Education Plus; An International Journal of Education & Humanities; APH Publishing Corporation, New Delhi; Vol XVI, No., 1, 2018.

• Area Of Interest is Population Studies And Statistical Methods.

ADDITIONAL: EXPERIENCE:

Programming in FORTRAN, Basic I worked in data analysis and Using Census Data. My books are sold on Amazon and Love Reading U K. I sent you the link by mail. I presented my paper in International Seminar organized by (PAA) Population Association of America 2021 Annual Meeting, "An Estimation of Fertility by Contraceptive Choice of Indian Couple" May 5-8, 2021.